Nonviolent Word

Nonviolent Word

Anabaptism, the Bible, and the Grain of the Universe

J. Denny Weaver
and
Gerald J. Mast

◆PICKWICK *Publications* • Eugene, Oregon

NONVIOLENT WORD
Anabaptism, the Bible, and the Grain of the Universe

Copyright © 2020 J. Denny Weaver and Gerald J. Mast. All rights reserved. Except for brief quotations in critical publications or reviews, no part of this book may be reproduced in any manner without prior written permission from the publisher. Write: Permissions, Wipf and Stock Publishers, 199 W. 8th Ave., Suite 3, Eugene, OR 97401.

Pickwick Publications
An Imprint of Wipf and Stock Publishers
199 W. 8th Ave., Suite 3
Eugene, OR 97401

www.wipfandstock.com

PAPERBACK ISBN: 978-1-7252-5701-6
HARDCOVER ISBN: 978-1-7252-5702-3
EBOOK ISBN: 978-1-7252-5703-0

Cataloguing-in-Publication data:

Names: Weaver, J. Denny, author. | Mast, Gerald J., author.

Title: Nonviolent Word : Anabaptism, the Bible, and the grain of the universe / by J. Denny Weaver and Gerald J. Mast.

Description: Eugene, OR: Pickwick Publications, 2020 | Includes bibliographical references and index.

Identifiers: ISBN 978-1-7252-5701-6 (paperback) | ISBN 978-1-7252-5702-3 (hardcover) | ISBN 978-1-7252-5703-0 (ebook)

Subjects: LCSH: Nonviolence—Religious aspects—Christianity | Anabaptists | Anabaptists—Doctrines | Marbeck Pilgram—approximately 1495–1556 | Menno Simons—1496–1561

Classification: BX4931 W43 2020 (print) | BX4931 (ebook)

The front cover image is derived from a drawing (*Page 37 Prime: Pages from the Manual for Dismantling God*) by artist and Bluffton University faculty member Philip Sugden depicting a Tibetan woman in spiritual awakening with the Hebrew text of Genesis 1:1–11 in the background.

Manufactured in the U.S.A.   02/21/20

To our students—who have questioned us,
challenged us, and given us hope.

Contents

Preface | ix

Introduction: The Word of God Is Solid Ground | 1

Part I. Early Anabaptists and the Nonviolent Word of God | 15

1. The Word of God in the *Ausbund* | 17
2. Marpeck's New Direction | 27
3. The Word of God in Menno's Christology | 42

Part II. Anabaptists and the Contemporary Believers Church | 61

4. The Nonviolent Grain of the Bible | 66
5. Black and White Believers Churches in Conversation | 86
6. Bearing Public Witness to the Gospel of Peace | 104

Conclusion: The Grain of the Universe as Figure and Entanglement | 133

Appendices

Appendix A: An Anabaptist Lectionary | 139
Appendix B: Trinitarian Terminology in the *Martyrs Mirror* | 144
Appendix C: Anabaptists and the Apocrypha | 148
Appendix D: Hymn by Michael Schneider | 151

Bibliography | 153
Subject Index | 161
Scripture Index | 167

Authors' Preface

THIS BOOK IS ANOTHER product of our long-standing and ongoing conversation about the meaning and significance of Anabaptism, both past and present. We began this conversation nearly a quarter of a century ago, when we first became colleagues at Bluffton University. Over the years we have collaborated on a variety of projects from planning conferences to editing essay collections to coauthoring essays and books, although many of our discussions about the prospects of Anabaptism have been the routine coffee conversation of friends who share common interests and commitments and who enjoy each other's company. One such coffee conversation led many years ago to our presentation of related papers on nonviolence in Anabaptist theology at an Anabaptist Colloquium at Eastern Mennonite University in 2006. Those papers eventually became chapters in a book entitled *Defenseless Christianity: Anabaptism for a Nonviolent Church*, which presented an argument for nonviolence as a defining platform for the historic Anabaptist communities that survived the conflicts of the European Reformation era. The present book is an extension of that discussion about nonviolence and Anabaptist theology into the field of Anabaptist biblical interpretation. Like its predecessor *Defenseless Christianity*, the book *Nonviolent Word* also has a section on the sixteenth century and a section for contemporary Anabaptists.

We tested the first chapter in each of these two sections of our book in three different venues during the 500th anniversary year of Martin Luther's publication of the 95 theses, generally regarded as the beginning of the Protestant Reformation. The papers were first previewed in a session of the 18th Believers Church Conference, "Word, Spirit and the Renewal of the Church," held at Goshen College in September 2017; then at Baylor University's annual Symposium on Faith and Culture in October 2017 that was focused on the theme of the Bible and the Reformation; and finally in a faculty colloquium at Bluffton University in November 2017. In addition, the chapter on "Black and White Believers Churches in Conversation" was presented in a different session of the Goshen conference.

For this book, Mast was the primary author of the introduction and chapters 1, and 3, and the conclusion, while Weaver produced the primary version of chapters 2, 4, 5, and 6. Both authors edited and approved all chapters.

We have received suggestions and support from other sources, as well. Ron Adams, Norris Glick, Angela Hicks, Coliér McNair, and Tim Peebles all reviewed parts of the book. While we have benefitted from all the feedback we have received, we acknowledge that the limits and blind spots in our thinking continue to be ours. Kathryn Roth and Olivia Westcott, research assistants in the art, communication and theatre department at Bluffton University, compiled the bibliography. Finally, we owe much to our families, who support our callings to think and write and teach on behalf of the church. We are grateful for this cloud of witnesses that surround us.

J. Denny Weaver and Gerald J. Mast,
Summer 2019

— INTRODUCTION —

The Word of God Is Solid Ground

THIS BOOK EXPLORES THE recovery of the Word of God as a concept that makes the life and teachings of Jesus Christ paradigmatic for understanding the truth of God and of God's creation. Beginning with the European Reformation, particularly the radical wing, the book explores how new understandings of biblical authority expressed in the language of that era have relevance now over five hundred years later when stated in contemporary idiom for evangelical, ecumenical, and anti-racist Christian witness.

An early Anabaptist song about the martyrdom of Hans van Overdam makes the confessional claim, "The Word of God is solid ground, our constant firm confession; no source of freedom more profound, no purer a profession."[1] This type of claim was not uncommon in the setting of the European Reformation—during which the technology of printing made the written Word of God in the Scriptures accessible to many commoners in their own language for the first time.[2] For many in the Reformation era, the words of Scripture became a source of great freedom from the institutions of Christendom that had monopolized scriptural interpretation in the hands of scholars and authorities who could read and discuss the Latin Vulgate.[3]

The rediscovery of the Bible in the Reformation era is sometimes compared to the finding of the book of the law during the reign of Josiah, king of Judah, as recorded in 2 Kings 22 and 23.[4] This neglected book

---

1. *Hymnal: A Worship Book*, #314. For the story of Hans van Overdam, see van Braght, *Bloody Theater; or, Martyrs Mirror*, 486–93.

2. Eisenstein, *Printing Revolution*, 148–86.

3. Ozment, *Protestants*, 192; Pelikan, *Reformation of the Bible*, 47–49.

4. See, for example, seventeenth-century Anglican priest John Mayer's commentary on 2 Kgs 22–23 as documented in Cooper and Lohrmann, *Reformation Commentary on Scripture*, 505. For a more recent example, see August Konkel's comment on 2 Chr 34–35 in the Believers Church Bible Commentary: "Martin Luther has a precedent in the story

of the law helped the people of Judah to remember the Lord their God whose rule they had disregarded and whose deliverance from slavery they had squandered. During the Reformation, the "book of the law" had been rediscovered in the words of the Bible that had been kept in the storage of monasteries and universities, unavailable for commoners to read and discuss. Using the new technologies of moveable type along with the knowledge of biblical languages, scholars like Martin Luther and William Tyndale gave the Scriptures to people at a price that many more could afford and in language they could understand and discuss and debate.[5] And in reading the Scriptures, many people realized that they had forgotten the ways of God and the Word of God.

The Reformation is sometimes thought to have begun on October 31, 1517, with Martin Luther's posting of ninety-five theses about the theology and practice of indulgences on the door of All Saints Church in Wittenberg. These theses went viral and led to the transformation of European Christendom. The first thesis in Luther's post says this: "Our Lord and Master Jesus Christ, in saying 'Do penance' wanted the entire life of the faithful to be one of penitence."[6]

Luther goes on to argue that the system of indulgences established by the church to monetize guilt trivialized the depth of God's judgment, as well as the endurance of God's everlasting mercy. God wants to restore our lives, now and forever, not just let us into heaven after we die by the skin of our teeth. God wants us to live in repentance, not just pay for our sin with money or good deeds. God means to put everything right in this world, not just keep chaos in check. This profound conviction discovered in the Scriptures about God's comprehensive justice and extravagant forgiveness is the central message of the Protestant Reformation. And the ground for this conviction is, as Luther acknowledged in theses 53 and 54, the hearing of the Word of God.[7]

We can see the Reformation era power of this knowledge of the Word of God in the life of Anabaptist bookseller Joriaen Simons—a story told in the *Martyrs Mirror*.[8] In a letter from prison that he wrote to his son,

---

of Josiah; it is a lesson on the importance of the written word as a power for Reform." Konkel, *1&2 Chronicles*, 437.

5. Eisenstein, *Printing Revolution*, 160–63.
6. Wengert, *Roots of Reform*, 34.
7. Wengert, *Roots of Reform*, 41.
8. Van Braght, *Bloody Theater; or, Martyrs Mirror*, 563–64.

he recalled the iniquity of his life before encountering the Word of God. He acknowledged having been proud, selfish, deceitful, and drunken. He confessed to having tried to seduce his neighbor's daughter. But then, he writes, he began to read the Scriptures and to "take the Word of God as my counselor."[9] This encounter with the Word of God completely changed Joriaen's life: "I abandoned my ease, voluntarily and uncompelled, and entered upon the narrow way, to follow Christ, my Head, well knowing that if I should follow him to the end, I should not walk in darkness."[10]

Joriaen's desire to be a new divine creature who had converted to a "pious, penitent, and godly life," led to his identification with the Anabaptist movement and to his imprisonment, along with Clement Dirks and Mary Joris in the Haarlem prison at St. John's gate in 1557. Mary Joris died while giving birth in prison. Clement and Joriaen were executed by fire on April 26, 1557, forty years after Luther posted the ninety-five theses.[11] According to the court order that is printed in the *Martyrs Mirror*, the Haarlem authorities condemned Clement and Joriaen because they had been rebaptized, because they held pernicious views about the sacraments and ceremonies of the church, and because they sold, read, and discussed false books.[12] The sentence of execution called them "disturbers of the common peace and of the Christian religion."[13]

Joriaen Simons, Clement Dirks, and Mary Joris were like many Christian believers in the Reformation era who heard the Word of God and obeyed it—as witnessed by the thousands of other testimonies in the *Martyrs Mirror*, but also in the martyr books of Catholics and Protestants during that violent and uncertain time.[14] For Protestants as well as for Anabaptists in the Reformation era, knowing the Word of God is closely identified with reading and hearing the Bible. In the words of Scripture, the Word of God speaks across the centuries, displaying the revelation of God's Word to people in changing settings and amid new challenges.[15]

---

9. Van Braght, *Bloody Theater; or, Martyrs Mirror*, 595.
10. Van Braght, *Bloody Theater; or, Martyrs Mirror*, 595.
11. Van Braght, *Bloody Theater; or, Martyrs Mirror*, 564.
12. Van Braght, *Bloody Theater; or, Martyrs Mirror*, 567.
13. Van Braght, *Bloody Theater; or, Martyrs Mirror*, 567.
14. For a comparative study of Catholic, Protestant, and Anabaptist martyrologies from the Reformation era, see Gregory, *Salvation at Stake*, 315–41.
15. For Protestants, "the unfolding of God's Word gives light (Ps 119:130), and the agency of the unfolding and light-giving is not the church or academic scholarship apart from the triune economy but rather the Spirit speaking (not just having spoken) in the

From this perspective, the covenant that God made with Abraham is a covenant that is also made with us when we read the Bible and receive God's promises (Gen 15). The message given by the angel of the Lord to Hagar is a promise of survival and significance that is good news for us as well when we find it in the Bible (Gen 16:10–12). The call Moses heard from the burning bush and the law he received on Mt. Sinai invite us through the Scriptures also to speak truth to power and to remember the Lord our God who brought us out of slavery from Egypt (Exod 3:10–12; 20:1–17). And the invitation to Mary of Nazareth to bear and birth the Son of God is an invitation to receive and offer Jesus Christ in our bodies and in our burdens (Luke 1:26–38). With Mary we may magnify the Lord and rejoice in God our Savior (Luke 1:46–56). And with the disciples, we are invited by Jesus Christ to lay down our lives and our weapons to follow after him (Matt 26:47–56).[16]

Indeed, the Word of God speaks to us in the Bible. But for Anabaptists like Joriaen Simons the Word of God is not limited to the words of Scripture. The Word of God is Jesus Christ, as revealed in Scripture, but also as revealed in the creation around us and in our own inner experiences of sacred knowledge. Hans Hut, for example wrote that in the thriving and suffering of the creatures all around us, "nothing is signified and preached other than Christ the crucified one alone, not only Christ the head but the whole Christ with all his members."[17] Hans Denck famously confessed that "Holy Scripture I hold above all human treasure but not as high as the Word of God that is living, powerful, and eternal—unattached and free of all the elements of this world."[18] For Denck, the Word of God is alive and on the loose and it will not be constrained by our theological management strategies. It will not stay between the covers of our Bibles—silent until

---

Scriptures (and through the church and, sometimes, the academy). It is God's own communicative action that is a lamp to our feet." Vanhoozer, *Biblical Authority*, 113.

16. This experience of the Word of God calling to us personally in the stories of the Bible involves what Karl Barth calls "appropriation." Such appropriation happens with integrity when we listen first for what a passage of the Bible is saying in its own historical and literary setting, followed by attention to what this message delivered then is reflecting to us now. When the reader of Scripture is then able to identify with the message of a scriptural witness, the Word of God can then be said to speak to the reader in particular: "Because the Word of God meets us in the form of the scriptural word, assimilation means the contemporaneity, homogeneity, and indirect identification of the reader and hearer of Scripture with the witness of the revelation." Barth, *Church Dogmatics*, I.2, 736.

17. Rempel, *Jörg Maler's Kunstbuch*, 122.

18. Bauman, *Spiritual Legacy of Hans Denck*, 251.

we bother to open them and begin to read. Denck's statement recalls the words of the writer of the book of Hebrews who describes the Word of God as living and active, sharper than any two edged sword (Heb 4:12). It will overtake us, finally, because it is the source of our life and will remain after our death—the hope of the resurrection.

The Word of God Creating, Dividing, Reconciling

At least three characteristics of this living and active Word of God shape Anabaptist understandings of the Bible—and the Bible's witness to "anyone who has ears to hear" of the Word made flesh—Jesus of Nazareth.[19] The Word creates, divides, and reconciles.

The Creating Word

First, we know from the biblical story of creation that the Word of God is a creating Word—the Word by which the Lord God spoke into existence the heavens and the earth (Gen 1). By the Word of God, a hundred billion galaxies and space itself exploded into being from nothing or next to nothing, expanding furiously from the infinitely dense and incomprehensibly tiny singularity that physicists believe contained all the mass and space and time that exists in the universe. By the Word of God, wiggling, kicking, and highly active bundles of life are birthed into existence from the desire that joins bodies and multiplies them. By the Word of God, texts are formed from letters, sentences from words, chapters from paragraphs, and the exploding and expanding and birthing universe is named and ordered and communicated through speech and writing and singing and painting and dancing.

Theologian Gordon Kaufman has suggested that this powerful and serendipitous creativity that brings worlds into existence—both in physical space and in our imaginative experiences—is the divine mystery to which we refer when we say the word God.[20] According to Kaufman, this divine mystery is expressed in the creativity and novelty displayed in the life and teachings of Jesus.[21] Kaufman's account of God as "serendipitous creativity" is a helpful

---

19. In the Synoptic Gospels, Jesus often concludes his teachings with a universal invitation: "Let anyone with ears to hear, listen!" (See Matt 11:15; Mark 4:9, 23; Luke 14:35).

20. Kaufman, *In Face of Mystery*, 264–73.

21. Kaufman, *Jesus and Creativity*, 27–61.

way of understanding the claims made in the first chapter of the Gospel of John that in Jesus Christ, the Word of God became flesh and dwelled among us. John's gospel says that from this Word of God that was enfleshed in Jesus Christ, all things came into being, and that what came into being through this word was life and light that the darkness will not overcome.

The writings of Menno Simons emphasize the power of this word to renew and restore. When the "seed of the divine Word" is sown into human hearts, this word "changes and renews the whole man, that is, from carnal to the spiritual, the earthly into the heavenly; it transforms from death unto life, from unbelief to belief and makes men happy. For through this seed all nations upon the earth are blessed."[22] The Word of God is indeed a creating and sustaining and enlightening and life-giving word.

The Dividing Word

The Word of God is also a dividing word. In creating the heavens and the earth, the Word of God separates light from darkness, day from night, and land from water. When God calls a people forth from the nations to be a light and a blessing, they are commanded to reject the practices of enslavement and violence practiced by the world's empires. From the prophet Isaiah and the Apostle Paul, the Word of God invites us: "Come out from among them and be ye separate, saith the Lord, and touch not the unclean thing, and I will receive you . . . and ye shall be my sons and daughters" (2 Cor 6:17 KJV).

Jesus confirms the divisiveness of the Word of God when he sends his disciples out to proclaim the good news in Matthew 10. He quotes the prophet Micah: "I have come to set a man against his father, and a daughter against her mother, and a daughter-in-law against her mother-in-law; and one's foes will be members of one's own household" (Matt 10:35–36). In a time of church conflict, many of us can confirm that the good news divides our families, but also our denominations: congregation against congregation, conference against conference, one's foes are members of one's own church family.

But, lest we become too confident that we are on the right side of gospel conflict, in the text from Hebrews 4 we learn that the Word of God not only sets people against each other, but that it gets inside of our very skin, turning us against ourselves "piercing until it divides soul from

---

22. Menno, *Complete Writings*, 57.

spirit, joints from marrow; it is able to judge the thoughts and intents of the heart" (v. 12). Much as we would like to hide the sin that clings to even our well-intended actions; much as we want to pretend to goodness, to life without guilt or confession, the dividing and judging Word of God will not rest until we are "naked and laid bare to the eyes of the one to which we must render an account" (v. 13).

In the biblical story of King Josiah and the recovery of the book of the law, the prophetess Huldah, like all faithful prophets, makes it clear that catastrophe follows from ignoring the Word of God: "Thus says the Lord: 'I will indeed bring disaster on this place because they have abandoned me and have made offerings to other gods'" (2 Kgs 22:16–17). The more mild-mannered Gordon Kaufman, in his book *Jesus and Creativity*, restates this judgment against human forgetfulness in a polite way: "We humans should always seek to live and act in response to the *creativity* going on in the world roundabout us and in our lives; for if we do not so live and act, we will soon be out of tune and out of touch with what is really happening in the world."[23] Gordon Kaufman is worried about the same catastrophe of forgetfulness as the prophetess Huldah, even though Kaufman speaks the language of academic theology and Huldah speaks Hebrew prophecy.

But the prophetess Huldah, like all faithful prophets, has good news to follow the bad news: "Because your heart was penitent, and you humbled yourself before the Lord . . . and because you have torn your clothes and wept before me . . . I will gather you to your ancestors, and you shall be gathered to your grave in peace; your eyes shall not see all the disaster that I will bring on this place" (2 Kgs 22:19–20). Martin Luther had it right, "Our Lord and Master Jesus Christ, in saying 'Do penance . . . ,' wanted the entire life of the faithful to be one of penitence." Joriaen Simons also was on the right track when he converted to a "pious, penitent, and godly life." Calling out and confessing sin is the faithful response to judgment and the first step toward the peace that the Word of God seeks to fulfill in the world.

We should acknowledge here that calling out and confessing the iniquities of our communities and of our own hearts leads to both peace and disaster. When we acknowledge the sin that has been uncovered by the Word of God, there is often conflict and suffering that follows. In the story of King Josiah's reformation, the response to the light of the law includes a great deal of interreligious violence: altars to the gods of the Moabites

---

23. Menno, *Complete Writings*, 8.

and the Samaritans are desecrated and their priests killed. In the woodcut from the *Martyrs Mirror* associated with the story of Joriaen Simons, we also see suffering and violence: Joriaen and Clement have been executed on the left, the priests and the magistrates are fleeing the riotous crowd of protesters in the background, and in the foreground, controversial books are being burned—no doubt some of them translations of the Bible considered to be false and heretical.

Execution of Joriaen and Clement, with book burning.

There is suffering in this image, yet also liberty: books and Bibles flying through the air like the birds of the sky, finding their way into the hands of readers hungry for knowledge, yearning to encounter God's Word written. What a dramatic picture of the dividing and discerning Word of God on the loose, inviting repentance and bringing both salvation and chaos!

The Reconciling Word

But the Word of God does not stop with the catastrophe of judgment. The Word of God is also and ultimately a reconciling word, a word that restores what has been broken and gathers what has been scattered. The story of Josiah's reformation anticipates this reconciliation even amid the killing of the priests and the raiding of shrines and tombs described at the end of 2 Kings 23. We read that during these raids one tomb was left alone: that of the man of God from Judah and the prophet from Samaria (vv. 17–18).

This is a reference to the story in 1 Kings 13 of a man of God from the southern kingdom of Judah visiting his enemies in the northern kingdom of Israel three hundred years earlier during the rule of Jeroboam. The man of God—a faithful Judean—prophesied that neglect of God would lead to disaster, including the destruction of the shrines and tombs at Bethel (vv. 1–3). Of course, King Jeroboam, like most people who are in charge of earthly kingdoms, did not much care for this kind of prophecy. He reached out his hand in anger toward the prophet from Judah and received a withered hand in return (v. 4). At this point his anger turned to repentance and thanks to the prayers of the prophet—prayers, indeed, for the prophet's enemy—the king's hand was restored (v. 6). When King Jeroboam invited the prophet from Judah to eat and drink with him, the prophet shunned him: no eating with the ungodly enemies in the north—those who would eventually be known as Samaritans (vv. 8–10).

But then the prophet from Judah received a second dinner invitation. An old prophet from Bethel invited him to share a meal (v. 15). At first the Judean prophet said no, but then, in a risky act of grace, gave up shunning and sat down together at the table to eat and drink with his enemy—the Bethel prophet (vv. 16–19). This cross-cultural act of reconciliation was indeed risky: a lion ended up killing the man of God from Judah before he could return home (v. 24). But, refusing to be defeated by violence and death, the prophet from Bethel buried the prophet from Judah in his own grave and requested to be buried with him at the time of his death (vv. 29–32). During the violence and destruction of Josiah's reformation, three hundred years later, the bones of these enemies who had become friends—Judaean and Samaritan—were left as they were, gathered together in their tomb, reconciled and at peace (2 Kgs 23:17–18).

This story—interpreted here in a way that emphasizes the divine and human impulse toward reconciliation even in the face of a perception that obedience to God demands shunning—is part of a thread of reconciliation that arguably winds through the entire Hebrew Bible. This thread includes confrontation with violence—as in God's challenge to Cain after he killed Abel: "Where is your brother Abel" (Gen 4:9)? The thread includes vulnerability to violence, such as with the figure of Joseph who is sold into slavery by his brothers (Gen 37). And the thread includes reconciliation, as in Joseph's forgiveness and embrace of his brothers (Gen 45) or the peace that Abigail negotiated between her husband Nabal and her future husband David (1 Sam 25).

Christians believe that the reconciling Word is made most visible in the life and teachings of Jesus Christ—a Jewish rabbi who famously shared water and conversation with a Samaritan woman and who loved and forgave his enemies, even unto his death on a cross. According to the writer of the epistle to the Ephesians, this crucified and resurrected body of Jesus Christ has become our peace, breaking down the dividing wall, putting to death hostility, and reconciling all of God's children to God in one body (Eph 2:13–16). By faith, we know that this reconciling word of God brings together those who have been divided: Jews and Gentiles, Christians and Muslims, Protestants and Catholics. And so we pray for the unity of the body of Christ even now, after nearly five hundred years of Reformation schism and division—some of which has illuminated the truth of God's Word and much of which has also led to violence and suffering and death.

We learn from Karl Barth that the Word of God not only reconciles hostile groups; it also makes peace within us, comforting and consoling and restoring our freedom. In the first volume of the great *Church Dogmatics*—which is focused on the doctrine of the Word of God—Barth reflects on what it means to bind ourselves to the Word of God. The Word of God bears our sins, when we confess and acknowledge them, and leaves us free from the anxiety that comes from the knowledge of good and evil. When we pray, "Thy will be done," according to Barth, we are admitting that "the burden of my own and of others' sins does not lie upon me. It lies solely and entirely upon Jesus Christ, upon the Word of God."[24]

Giving our lives over to the Word of God is a defining act of freedom, one that accepts the Word of God as a trustworthy and reliable counselor, just as Joriaen Simons did. When we turn our lives over to the Word of God in this way our relationship with the Word of God, Jesus Christ, becomes personal and, to use Barth's words, "consists always in our knowing and saying and confirming and attesting and living out the truth: that He careth for you."[25]

From this standpoint, the whole point of reading and studying and discussing the Bible is to become acquainted with the birth, life, ministry, teachings, death, resurrection, and ascension of Jesus Christ—the one

---

24. Barth, *Church Dogmatics*, I.2, 275.
25. Barth, *Church Dogmatics*, I.2, 275.

who cares for us and accepts our burdens. This acquaintance and care is confirmed in our experience of the created world around us as a great gift of God's love—an expression of the same vulnerable and unqualified love that is displayed in Jesus Christ—both in his confrontation with violence ("put your sword back into its place for all who take the sword will perish by the sword" [Matt 26:52]) and his embrace of the enemy ("forgive them for they do not know what they are doing" [Luke 23:34]). And we come to know Jesus as our own inner desires and affections become aligned with the love and passion of Jesus Christ in the visible life of Christ's body—the church—in its Spirit-guided mission of peace and reconciliation. When we come to know Jesus Christ in this way, we also realize that the Word of God is above all else a living and loving word—a peaceable word. Although this peaceable Word judges and discerns and is thus often greeted with violence, it is a mistake to attribute violence itself to the Word of God. The Word of God is a light that actively dispels the shadows and thus can be understood to wage a certain kind of "war against the powers" of this world, as Greg Boyd has explained in his masterful work on the overcoming of violence in the biblical narrative.[26]

But although the Word of God is a powerful force that consumes and overcomes evil, the struggle of life and truth over death and lies that the Word of God advances does not itself engage in violence, even though the Bible uses metaphors of conflict and warfare to describe this struggle against evil. The Word of God is instead the good with which we are called to overcome evil: the truth that exposes lies and the life that overcomes death. That is not to say that the Word of God lacks creativity when it comes to the confrontation with violence. As Greg Boyd explains, the creativity of the Word of God allows the violence of evil to constrain and punish evil, to self-annihilate. The Word of God deals with the forces of evil and violence through a vengeance of consuming judgment—allowing the sword to destroy the sword, armies to wipe out armies, and conquest to overthrow conquest.[27]

---

26. Boyd, *Crucifixion of the Warrior God*, 1075–81.

27. This idea of "Aikido-like" judgment on sword-wielding is from Boyd, *Crucifixion of the Warrior God*, 984–87.

INTRODUCTION: THE WORD OF GOD IS SOLID GROUND

The Word of God and the Grain of the Universe

The creating, dividing, and reconciling Word of God is solid ground, "no source of freedom more profound," to recall again the words of the old Anabaptist hymn cited at the beginning of this introduction. That conviction shapes the chapters in this book, which are organized into two main sections. Part 1 develops several testimonies from Anabaptists of the sixteenth century about the defenseless or nonviolent power of the word of God—as revealed in the Bible's witness to the life of Jesus Christ, in the humanity of Christ as expressed in a defenseless church, and in the inner experiences and social practices of faithful believers. These chapters cover a range of early European Anabaptist literature—from the Swiss Brethren hymnal—the *Ausbund*—to the writings of South German leader Pilgram Marpeck to the work of Dutch and North German leader Menno Simons. In these chapters, it is clear that Anabaptist writers used a variety of images to depict the Word of God in Scripture and as made present in Jesus Christ. The chapters in part 2 continue that expansive practice.

Part 2 deals with the contemporary and ecumenical usefulness of Anabaptist conceptions of the Word of God in three venues of the church's witness: its ongoing interpretation of the Bible through ecumenical conversation, its struggle to reflect the reconciling Word of God in the challenge against racism and white supremacy, and its active social witness against violence of all kinds. The predominant metaphor used in part 2 for the Word of God is the phrase "the grain of the universe."[28] This phrase captures our specific understanding of the Word of God as the creative power that both establishes and sustains the cosmos in a manner that reflects the peaceable character of Jesus Christ. It is this sense in which we argue for a "peaceable Word"—that is a word that invites and appeals and judges and condemns but that does not coerce or demand or harm or kill.

To say that the Word is peaceable or nonviolent or defenseless is not to say that it is powerless. To the contrary, we accept the biblical witness to what the Apostle Paul called "the wisdom of the cross." According to this

---

28. The phrase "the grain of the universe" is derived from the statement John Howard Yoder made that "the point that apocalyptic makes is not only that people who wear crowns and who claim to foster justice by the sword are not as strong as they think—true as that is: we still sing, 'O where are Kings and Empires now of old that went and came?' It is that people who bear crosses are working with the grain of the universe." Yoder, "Armaments and Eschatology," 58. Stanley Hauerwas used this phrase as the title of his 2000–2001 Gifford Lectures, published as *With the Grain of the Universe*.

wisdom, "God chose what is foolish in the world to shame the wise; God chose what is weak in the world to shame the strong; God chose what is low and despised in the world, things that are not, to reduce to nothing things that are" (1 Cor 2:26–28). We see this profound claim by Paul about the wisdom and weakness of the cross as the key to understanding both the challenging truth of the Bible and the deepest meaning of the universe. In Jesus Christ, God was and is reconciling the world; if anyone is in Christ— there is a new creation—this is the essential witness of Scripture, both of the canonical Bible and of creation's book (2 Cor 5:17–19).

This understanding of the Word of God as a weak yet enabling and flourishing word reflects a recovery of what Grace Jantzen has called "an imaginary of natality" and that Mayra Rivera names "a poetics of flesh." Jantzen and Rivera seek to resituate human flourishing within the soil—the "solid ground" if you will—of the physical and material world that gives birth to human bodies and that sustains them. Rather than posing the creativity of the word against the bodies it creates or transcends, this feminist approach to the Word of God aligns with the word's enfleshment and with the birthing and flourishing and healing of bodies and flesh.[29]

J. Kameron Carter, following the church father Irenaeus, has shown how the flesh of Jesus Christ "recapitulates" the flesh of Adam and of Israel—the locus of creation and flourishing in the Hebrew Bible. This recapitulation of creation and exodus in the flesh of Jesus Christ imprints a "new modality of existence" on the creation, a "modality of the cross" that "refuses to tyrannically possess the world."[30] Carter's theological work helps us to free our understandings of the Word of God from ideologies of whiteness and white supremacy that imagine a saving word unencumbered by the flesh and color of bodies—a white word. As such, the weakness of the word—and therefore its power and authenticity—is defined by the vulnerable flesh and color and sex of the word. This, too, is what we mean by invoking the "grain of the universe" as a metaphor for describing the cross-shaped Word in its material and cosmic reality in part 2 of this book.

The book provides several appendices of practical resources in Christian formation that reflect this focus on the wisdom of the cross as the central meaning of the Bible and of the cosmos. One item is an Anabaptist lectionary drawn from two historic lectionaries of the Anabaptist tradition. This lectionary demonstrates one way to routinely read and interpret Scripture in

---

29. Jantzen, *Becoming Divine*, 145–55; Rivera, *Poetics of Flesh*, 20–23.
30. Carter, *Race*, 27–28.

a way that privileges the life and teachings of Jesus Christ as recorded in the Synoptic Gospels, while treating the rest of the biblical canon as a literary horizon that contextualizes Jesus' life and teachings. Other appendices address the way Anabaptists interpreted the Bible in their response to Trinitarian arguments as found in testimonies collected in the *Martyrs Mirror*, and the generous Anabaptist use of the biblical texts referred to by Protestants as the Apocrypha and by Catholics as the deuterocanonical books.

Together, the chapters and appendices of this book display one distinct Anabaptist way to receive the Word of God as disclosed in Scripture. This word and grain is, we believe, a reliable and solid ground for faith and life in a time of struggle and transformation, whether that time is the Protestant reformation or our own turbulent era. And it speaks to all Christians who are committed to Jesus Christ as their example, ruler, and savior.

Part One

Early Anabaptists and the Nonviolent Word of God

CHAPTER 1

The Word of God in the *Ausbund*

THIS CHAPTER FOCUSES ON the vision of the Word of God as expressed in the hymns of the *Ausbund*—a collection of Anabaptist songs and martyr ballads published in the sixteenth century, the earliest known edition of which came out in 1565. The *Ausbund*—in its various editions—has been in continuous use during the past four hundred and fifty years and continues to be the primary hymnbook used by the Amish in their worship services.

The distinct picture of the Word of God found in the *Ausbund* is expressed well in the seventy-fifth hymn, which is attributed to Walpurga von Pappenheim, a friend of Anabaptist leader Pilgram Marpeck and a member of his spiritual circle.[1] The von Pappenheims were a noble family with numerous ties to Anabaptist and spiritualist conventicles, beginning in the 1530s, including three women who gave up their wealth and privilege to become attached to the Marpeck group.[2]

The writer of this song—whose authorship is somewhat contested—develops a picture of authentic Christian faith that confirms the choices made by the von Pappenheim women.[3] Those with a "believing heart" are said in this song to offer their lives to the grace of God, including their "property, goods, and body," hoping that God will, "to his praise, change our whole walk of life."[4]

This loving God to whom those with a "believing heart" give their lives is described in this song as an exclusively merciful, forgiving, and sustaining divinity: "He loves us and is gracious to us, mercifully forgiving us

---

1. *Ausbund*, 351–53.

2. Hege et al., "Pappenheim, Marschalk von," 115–16.

3. For a discussion that attributes the song to Michael Weisse, see Wolkan, *Die Lieder der Wiedertäufer* 123–25.

4. *Ausbund*, 351–53.

every debt, making us to be overcomers." He "gives us his good Spirit who renews our hearts" and who helps us "do what he bids."[5]

In the second to last stanza of the song, the songwriter asks for this loving God's help amid the distress and poverty of persecution and prays for the clarifying power of the Word of God. "Enlighten us with your radiant Word (hellen Wort), that in this dark place no false light may blind us."[6] In the final stanza, the songwriter connects the light of God's Word with the simplicity of singing, asking God to "accept as praise" what "we sing in simplicity" and to "give your Word with a clear sound" that will "pierce through the hearts" and empower the believers to "attain the crown of life."[7]

Although its nine stanzas make it one of the shorter hymns in the *Ausbund*, this hymn summarizes well a distinct Anabaptist doctrine of the Word of God that is expressed throughout the many songs collected in the 1583 edition of the *Ausbund*, as well as in the editor's preface to the 1583 edition. Although these songs originate from all of the distinct regions of Anabaptist activity—from Switzerland to South and Central Germany to the Netherlands—they share in common a picture of the Word of God as an empowering and creative force that flows from a primarily peaceable God whose will is expressed most definitively in the life and teachings of Jesus Christ as found in the Bible and displayed in the faithful church.

Like many Protestant writers who celebrate the authority of the Word of God, *Ausbund* hymns frequently refer to the Word of God as a brilliant and discerning light that exposes falsehood and reveals divine truth. In this chapter we will focus on three other prominent characterizations that appear repeatedly in *Ausbund* hymns and support distinctive Anabaptist understandings: the Word of God as a spiritual seed, reliable ground and un-coercive gift. These metaphors each reinforce the relationship between the nonviolence of the Word of God and the transformative power of that Word in the Anabaptist theology presented in the *Ausbund*.

God's Word as Spiritual Seed

The *Ausbund* songwriters repeated a common Anabaptist understanding that the Word of God was a spiritual seed planted in the body of Mary, which gave birth not only to Jesus Christ but through Jesus Christ to a new

5. *Ausbund*, 352.
6. *Ausbund*, 353.
7. *Ausbund*, 353.

humanity, capable of righteousness and holiness. The unknown writer of song number 67, for example, identifies Jesus Christ as the Word of Truth, but also as the Father of the new humanity (*neuen Menschen*).[8] For this new humanity, the old flesh is made new in baptism, reborn into the New Jerusalem, and taught by the Spirit.

The hymn develops the image of the new person as a child of the Trinity: "one God, three names, from whom comes a child of God, washed entirely clean from sin."[9] This sanctified child acts in the "name and nature of Christ" and in the "Spirit of our Lord" to "turn all things unto Christ," becoming the enemy of sin and uniting with God.[10] In order to mature in the Christian life, the newborn person exercises vigorously in God's Word (*In Gottes Wort sich herzlich übt*), which is nourishment and life leading to fruits of faith.[11] These fruits of faith in the maturing Christian include triumphing over the world and sin, sharing in the breaking of bread and washing of feet, showing love to neighbors with deeds, and being peaceable (*Friedsam*) with everyone.[12]

Moreover, the new person born of Christ attends to his or her personal mission (*Sendung*), including the possibility of being a minister, and entrusts all material goods to God.[13] Following this "summary of Christian conduct" the song moves toward its conclusion, acknowledging the controversial nature of its teaching and anticipating objections: "If anyone understands Christ more deeply, and can provide a better teaching, they should instruct us . . . on the basis of Holy Scripture. Otherwise leave us alone."[14]

This song clearly distinguishes the Word of God or the Word of Truth, which is Jesus Christ, from the Holy Scriptures that bear witness to Jesus Christ and to which we are accountable in our search together to know Christ more deeply and to follow Christ more obediently. The Word is what regenerates us; the Bible is what disciplines us—the source of better teaching and deeper instruction.

In another *Ausbund* song (#70), Sigmund von Bosch—also a friend of Marpeck's—combines the incarnational theology found in John 1 with

---

8. *Ausbund*, 308.
9. *Ausbund*, 308.
10. *Ausbund*, 308–9.
11. *Ausbund*, 309.
12. *Ausbund*, 309–10.
13. *Ausbund*, 310–11.
14. *Ausbund*, 311.

the infancy narrative in Luke 2. Bosch describes Jesus Christ as the "true grain of wheat, sown in the earth" and as the Word of God joined with the seed of David and of Abraham.[15] In the unfolding images of the song, this partnership of the spiritual Word with human flesh defines Jesus Christ, who became one new man from two (v. 19), who redeems us "in our earthly flesh and blood," and who makes us "members of his body" through the marriage of Christ and the church.[16] Bosch's song gives attention to the role of Mary in the incarnation; she is a "pure woman," the virgin to whom the Word of God came, the flesh to whom the Spirit was joined to conceive the "Tender One"—Jesus Christ.[17] Because he has our flesh, this new human—Jesus Christ—is able to help us and have compassion on us. Because "we are of his flesh," we can believe and be "devoted to God."[18] In this way, the Word brings life, awakens us, and "brings us into Heaven."[19]

Such images of the Word of God as a generative seed and defining power—somewhat similar to Menno's understanding of the Word of God as an incorruptible seed (see chapter 3) make it clear that an encounter with the Word of God not only clarifies the truth but brings forth new life and new capacities. For *Ausbund* song writers and singers, the Word of God is what makes all things new, including our very humanity.

God's Word as Solid Ground

Not only does the Word of God regenerate believers, in the spiritual world of the *Ausbund* it also offers secure footing for a life of faith and risk. Among the few *Ausbund* songs translated into attractive English verse and set to a singable melody is the "The Word of God Is Solid Ground," a song that comes from the Dutch Anabaptist songbook *Het Offer Des Heeren* (*The Sacrifice of the Lord*) and that commemorates the martyrdom of Hans van Overdam, executed at Ghent on July 9, 1551.[20] This song expresses that "whoever confesses God's Word must endure much suffering" and "will be hated at all times" just like Hans the cheese merchant from Amsterdam.[21]

15. *Ausbund*, 332.
16. *Ausbund*, 335.
17. *Ausbund*, 331–32.
18. *Ausbund*, 336.
19. *Ausbund*, 336.
20. *Hymnal: A Worship Book*, #314.
21. *Ausbund*, 72.

People like Hans have found a good foundation—solid ground—in God's Word, which they proclaim joyfully, even while facing imprisonment, interrogation, and execution. The truth of God's Word is reliable even when the house of justice is perverted and the Emperor becomes an adversary. Hans's testimony is that "whatever God's Word brings forth, to this I hold fast," no matter what the Emperor commands or forbids.[22] The emperor, said Hans, has no authority to govern the conscience."[23]

These claims about the reliability of God's Word are placed within a dramatic narrative of dissent against the religious and political establishment and offer a picture of the Word of God as solid leverage against the vengeful powers of this world. Even though the world attacks and persecutes, those who confess the Word of God will be led from suffering to eternal joy through Jesus Christ.[24] Such an image of the Word as ground or foundation emphasizes less the epistemological dimension of the Word's reliability and more the ontological security of its power: The Word of God will not let us down. We can trust our lives with it, even when it means taking on the Emperor and the house of justice.

Another Dutch Anabaptist martyr, Anna Jansz of Rotterdam, echoes this confidence in the Word of God amid the insecurity of the world. Those who follow the Lamb wherever it goes, who despise the pomp and pleasure of this world, and who carry the cross of Christ, these are those who keep the Word of God and are therefore without a secure dwelling place. In the words attributed to Anna Jansz, when the Word of God strips away all worldly sources of safety from believers, they become a home for God: "God dwells with such people, who are mocked by the world; do join yourself to them."[25] In other words, the Word of God dwells with those who have no dwelling except for the Word of God.

This understanding of the Word of God as a solid ground aligns with an acceptance of Holy Scripture as a reliable source of this knowledge of the Word of God. In hymn 67 cited earlier, for example, the writer invites instruction in the deeper ways of Christ, but only insofar as it is "founded on the Holy Scripture."[26] Another song is a memoir of Hans von Bilach, whose encounter with death leads him to amend his life, to sneak off to

---

22. *Ausbund*, 74.
23. *Ausbund*, 75.
24. *Ausbund*, 77.
25. *Ausbund*, 99.
26. *Ausbund*, 311.

church (*Gmeine*): "Here I found God's Word spoken, to the poor as to the rich, they taught out of the Holy Scriptures" (48:5).[27]

God's Word as Nonviolent Gift

Perhaps the most thoroughly developed distinctive Anabaptist image of the Word of God is its nonviolence—the way it is offered to us as a gift without threat or demand by contrast with the Word's corruption by the authorities who seek to impose it through the sword. This principle of the Word's nonviolence is articulated already in the hymn written by Felix Mantz—the first Anabaptist martyr in Zurich. The hymn notices that many people proclaim the Word of God and yet stand in "hate and envy, having no godly love."[28] These false prophets and wolves in sheep's clothing "call upon the authorities that they should kill us."[29] By contrast, Christ in his patience "compels no one," "accuses no one," and "hates no one."[30] According to Mantz, only "love will surely prevail"—the "pure love of Christ" that is "merciful to the adversary."[31]

That this characteristic of nonviolence or noncoercion is a defining feature of the spirituality expressed in this song collection is confirmed by editor's preface to the 1583 edition. In this preface, the editor begins by insisting that faith is "not a result of human custom, or coercion, or willing, or doing, but rather it is a gift of God's mercy, yes, a spiritual gift of God, sent down from above," and a "spiritual inscription of the Spirit of Christ on the minds and hearts of those who have entered into the new covenant."[32]

As the preface continues, the editor explains one practical implication of this understanding of faith as uncoerced: "For no one will be forced to believe anything, other than what seems to correspond with Scripture, unlike what one sees with many today, against (the teachings) of Scripture."[33] The editor points out that "many confess through coercion, or hypocrisy, or to attain favor" and many sow their seed "through the punishment of

---

27. *Ausbund*, 233–34.
28. *Ausbund*, 37.
29. *Ausbund*, 38.
30. *Ausbund*, 38–40.
31. *Ausbund*, 39.
32. *Ausbund*, 2; translation in Snyder, *Later Writings*, 135.
33. *Ausbund*, 2; Snyder, *Later Writings*, 135.

sword, prison, or money."[34] Such confessing and planting return no fruit because human beings are taking "what belongs to God's office"; in other words, "that which is driven by (God's) Spirit and should be accepted with willing hearts, is forced onto people by fleshly coercion."[35]

For the 1583 *Ausbund* editor, any effort to enforce faith by circumscribing how one reads Scripture, corrupts faith and results in fruitlessness. By contrast, genuine faith is freely received and enacted, a "gift of God's mercy."[36]

In the first song of the 1583 *Ausbund* written by Sebastian Franck, a spiritualist understanding of the nonviolent Word of God is applied to the practice of singing. Franck distinguishes between those who hear the Word with their ears and move their mouths in response, on the one hand, from those who sing in the Spirit and from the heart. According to Franck, "Only the heart can sing what rings true before God, your mouth is but an interpreter" so that "your heart is grounded as your mouth moves in the law of the Lord."[37] Without this grounding in God's law as known in the heart, the mouth simply becomes a "work without faith" uttering "empty flattery" and "perfecting syllables, sounding forth without spirit, going about only in form."[38] Franck's lyrics urge singers to "be cleansed first, learn to do good, practice righteousness and mercy, love your neighbor," and then to express these righteous intentions at first in silent prayer that does not move the lips and then in joyful praise that overflows from the lips.[39] All of this reflects a spiritualist understanding that prefers the inner spiritual motivation over the outer imposed practice as the authentic ground of faith.

To summarize the teachings about the nonviolence of God's Word in the *Ausbund*: the Word of God is given; it does not coerce and it does not impose. Unlike the corrupt and coercive practices of the established churches that force people to accept what they do not willingly embrace, authentic faith is grounded in the given and received Word of God. This noncoercive Word is fittingly sung as a spiritual song—an expression of what is authentically experienced in the heart; not simply mouth religion or saying what is expected or imposed.

---

34. *Ausbund*, 2–3; Snyder, *Later Writings*, 135.
35. *Ausbund*, 3–4; Snyder, *Later Writings*, 136.
36. *Ausbund*, 2; Snyder, *Later Writings*, 135.
37. *Ausbund*, 3.
38. *Ausbund*, 3–4.
39. *Ausbund*, 2.

These characterizations of the Word of God as light and seed and ground and gift shaped the way Anabaptists who sang these songs used and interpreted the Bible. For example, these metaphors shaped their reception of Scripture as a source of knowledge about Jesus Christ. Following in the path of patristic and medieval traditions of biblical interpretation that feature what Grace Jantzen calls the "mystical meaning of scripture," the writers and singers of *Ausbund* hymns assumed that the Word of God is Jesus Christ and that "everything in Scripture" points to Christ, not just in the literal historical sense but also in the figurative and poetic sense.[40]

The metaphor of light helped Anabaptists to understand Jesus Christ as the light that shines forth from Scripture. The metaphor of seed helped them to understand Jesus Christ as the seed sown in the earth of humanity that bears fruit in the resurrected life. The metaphor of ground emphasized the reliability of Jesus Christ as a source of strength and truth. The metaphor of gift stressed that the Word of God is not imposed and cannot be assimilated to worldly power and coercion.

This figurative knowledge of the Word of God is innovative and fruitful in the sense that it provides leverage for dissent from various forms of established Christendom. But it is also a traditional method of reading the Bible that shares more in common with Catholic monastic and contemplative practices than with the nominalism that shaped Protestant reform. For the Anabaptists who composed, compiled, and sang *Ausbund* hymns, all of Scripture bears witness to the life of Jesus Christ and therefore also to the calling of Christ's disciples. This life of Christ and of the believer is the deep meaning of Scripture, confirmed by the details of biblical literature, as well as by the particulars of the cosmos displayed in everyday creaturely life. Moreover, this Christian life when displayed as collective obedience to the rule of Christ becomes the Word of God made visible in community—in the *Gemeinde*—not just as a sermon delivered from the preacher's pulpit but as a witness exhibited by the gathered body. Such a collective witness includes teaching and baptizing new believers, sharing in the Lord's Supper, and serving one another, as well as singing together in un-coerced spiritual solidarity.

This conflict inviting and possession abandoning collective witness is possible because the Word of God to which it testifies and by which it exists is Jesus Christ. In an essay on Menno Simons and Karl Barth published in 1961, J. A. Oosterban, who taught theology at the Mennonite Seminary in

---

40. Jantzen, *Power, Gender, and Christian Mysticism*, 68.

Amsterdam, claimed that "the Bible for Menno Simons was the revelation of God in Christ Jesus, nothing more and nothing less."[41] Jesus Christ is the basis for the unity we find in Scripture—not some balance of Old and New Testament or an abstract theological system that we can imagine to exist behind or underneath Scripture. Jesus Christ constitutes the unity of Scripture because Jesus Christ is himself an inseparable unity, according to Oosterban. That is because the eternal Word of God who was with God in the beginning at the creation is identified with the Jesus Christ who became flesh: "The Christ of creation is the same as the Christ of the atonement."[42] Because the one who creates is also the one who saves, writes Oosterban, believers are able to experience not just "a relative improvement of one's moral life," but rather a "radical renewal of one's entire person."[43] Of course, that radical regeneration of the new flourishing humanity by the Word of God Jesus Christ is the joyful proclamation of the songwriters and singers of the *Ausbund*, from beginning to end.

A Concluding Hymn

In order to sense more fully how Anabaptist songwriters and singers expressed both the solid confidence in the Word of God that characterized Luther's Reformation and the specific Anabaptist vision of that Word as the enduring and sacrificial love of Jesus Christ from beginning to end, this chapter concludes with one of the fifty-three core *Ausbund* songs that were written and sung in the Passau prison between 1535 and 1537.[44] Nearly sixty men and women affiliated with Philip Plener's Anabaptist community in Moravia had been imprisoned at Passau following the expulsion of the Philipites and other Anabaptist groups from Moravia following the catastrophe at Münster. Like many Anabaptist conventicles the Philipites were clearly a singing church and the leaders of the imprisoned group at Passau were also songwriters. This hymn by Michael Schneider is one of thirteen that he contributed to the fifty-three songs in the Passau section of the *Ausbund*.

This song is also one of three *Ausbund* hymns for which Luther's great Reformation composition *Ein Feste Berg* is the suggested tune. I (Gerald)

---

41. Oosterban, "Theology of Menno Simons," 190.
42. Oosterban, "Theology of Menno Simons," 192.
43. Oosterban, "Theology of Menno Simons," 194.
44. For more on the Passau songs in the *Ausbund*, see Mast, "Suffering Mission in the Passau Songs."

have translated and versified three of the twenty-two stanzas of this Anabaptist hymn that continues to be sung by the Amish in connection with the reading of 1 Corinthians 13 in their lectionary schedule.

As you read these words, imagine yourself singing Luther's "A Mighty Fortress" but with these words instead. Imagine that you are singing these words inside a fortress that imprisons you. Let Luther's bold tune drive Michael Schneider's Anabaptized theology of the cross—a theology of the defenseless and enduring Word of God:

> 1. (1)
> O Lord God ruling from your throne,
> Your laws and statutes gave us
> A way to live for you alone
> Released from selfish blindness.
> But now through Jesus Christ, we who have been baptized
>   Know only one command: to love without demand;
> God's call to gracious service.
>
> 2. (14)
> Against all strife and tyranny
>   God's love for us is given.
> This love endures defenselessly
>   Though death and devil threaten.
> Because of Jesus Christ, our discord harmonized.
>   We fear not any foe; when love is all we know,
> No conflict can dishearten.
>
> 3. (18)
> Sisters and brothers let us take
>   The path to joy from sorrow.
> The cross of costly friendship make
>   Our past and our tomorrow.
> We follow Jesus Christ, who gave for us his life;
>   Came here with us to dwell, delivered us from hell,
> Through fierce and faithful mercy.[45]

---

45. *Ausbund*, 386–92. See Appendix D for Schneider's hymn with the score of Luther's tune.

CHAPTER 2

Marpeck's New Direction

Sixteenth-century Anabaptists set in motion a churchly trajectory whose implications we are still understanding and developing. This new churchly direction claimed the story of Jesus as the ultimate norm or reference point for faith and practice. With this norm, what began as a movement to reform the practice of baptism, developed into a church that not only rejected the established church but became a witness to or a challenge to the social order.

This chapter explores the way the new trajectory is visible in the theological writings of Pilgram Marpeck. More specifically, the thesis is that Marpeck developed theology that was first of all specific to Jesus rather than merely building on the classic christological formulas and filling them in with Anabaptist emphases. In arguing that Marpeck's theology reflects his new, Anabaptist orientation, this chapter disputes the conclusion that he had a classic, trinitarian orientation.[1]

The discussion involves two related foci. One concerns his comments—some very caustic—about the Catholic and Lutheran churches he rejected. It seems illogical to think that he would forcefully reject the inherited church and its trust in the sword, yet retain its theology for his peace church. The other focus concerns his own doing of theology. Marpeck emerges from this discussion as one who wrote theology specific to Jesus.

---

1. On Anabaptists as some version of "orthodox" and classical trinitarian, see Blough, *Christ in Our Midst*; Rempel, in Marpeck, *Later Writings*, 17, 72; references throughout Rempel, *Lord's Supper in Anabaptism*; and Rempel, "Critically Appropriating," 59–75; Finger, *Contemporary Anabaptist Theology*, 376, 381, 433, 434; Klaassen and Klassen, *Marpeck*, 344.

Pilgram Marpeck's Distinct Theological Direction

This section of the chapter analyzes the way Marpeck did theology. These writings reveal both his distinct Anabaptist orientation and reflect his political and religious context.

Exposé of the Babylonian Whore

Marpeck's tract *Exposé of the Babylonian Whore* displays clearly his distance from both the inherited Catholic tradition and the evangelical or Lutheran preachers who had first brought him to challenge papal error. It was published twice. Both appearances were provoked by Protestant preparations for military action against Catholics. Its appearance in late 1531 was a response to the formation of the Schmalkaldic League, which Strasbourg joined in February of 1531. This league was an alliance of Protestant princes to confront militarily the Catholic princes and the imperial forces loyal to Charles V. The reappearance of the tract in 1544 corresponded to recent fighting between the Schmalkaldic League and an alliance of forces of Charles V. Marpeck strongly opposed the Lutheran argument that God had given believing Christians the duty to wield the sword for the government in resisting evil and defending the gospel. The republication of *Exposé* served both to remind Protestants of the harm that accompanied rebellion against constituted authority, and to strengthen the commitment to nonviolence among Marpeck's Anabaptist followers.[2]

As Marpeck explains in *Exposé*, true Christians follow the "patience of Christ," which means to submit to authority rather than to rebel against it. In Marpeck's Anabaptist view, patient believers could protest against and admonish a wicked government.[3] Furthermore, by bearing the cross as a public witness, believers resist the enemies of Christ and bring about long term or eternal victory, if not short term safety or success.[4] However, rather than rebelling or violently resisting it, followers of Christ are to submit patiently to its oppression. Thus both Protestants and Anabaptists, Marpeck argues, should submit to Charles V, the highest constituted authority.

---

2. Klaassen and Klassen, *Marpeck*, 156–58, 278–79.
3. Marpeck, "Exposé," 29.
4. Marpeck, "Exposé," 29–30.

Marpeck writes that events unfolding before their eyes are exposing the wickedness of the world, which is witnessed to by Scripture.[5] The wickedness is the Lutheran claim that opposing the emperor militarily aligns with the will of Christ. He likens this claim to the whore of Revelation 17 that is being boldly exposed "like a secret adulteress who for a long time deceived her husband under a false cloak of pious faithfulness." In contrast to the "little flock," namely Marpeck's Anabaptists who reveal the power of God in their weakness, the "villainous whore" has "not hesitated to make unclean and to defile that glory by means of many temptations and errors which emerge from the heart of the community of the faithful."[6] One stratagem of the Protestant whore, whom Marpeck conflated with the "dragon and old serpent" of Rev 20:2, was to deceive people into believing that infant baptism, opposition to the pope's view of Lord's Supper, and communion in both kinds were the issues on which salvation depended. They were "whitewashing" the Scriptures so that "princes, the nobility and the cities" such as Strasbourg were led to oppose the emperor militarily. As a result God will bring "great bloodshed" on all because of "the false prophets and their supporters."[7]

Against these rebellious Protestants, Marpeck holds up the example of Jesus, the "crucified, patient, and loving Christ." He was "subject to all Authority and never responded with violence. Even so today we must not resist." Earthly authority has power over all things except vengeance, which belongs to God alone. Christ does not distribute earthly or imperial power. His followers respond with "patience and love" whether or not they are treated with justice. This patience is required because true faith cannot be coerced. Thus Marpeck sums up, "I present the so-called evangelicals and their teachers and preachers no other alternative than the crucified, patient, and loving Christ."[8] In other words, the norm for identifying the actions of Jesus' followers is the story and actions of Jesus. What is definitive about Jesus Christ is that he rejected the use of the sword and submitted to authority; his followers are to do likewise.

Marpeck acknowledged the role that these evangelical preachers had once played in helping him come to the truth. Through their teaching he came to oppose papal error. But now he faults these same evangelicals

---

5. Marpeck, "Exposé," 24.
6. Marpeck, "Exposé," 25.
7. Marpeck, "Exposé," 26–27.
8. Marpeck, "Exposé," 27.

for being skillful preachers of a Christ without a cross. It does not work, Marpeck says, to preach Christ and simultaneously to defend use of the sword. "What is missing in their teaching is the cross of Christ; they resist it and teach others to resist it." They preach a Christ without a cross, and "take refuge behind princes, lords, and cities." Marpeck calls this "the teaching and kingdom of Antichrist," and it must be opposed[9] since God has appointed civil authority (Rom 13). Therefore, even if civil authority rules unjustly or protects wickedness, the servants of God must leave vengeance to God. They may "admonish that Authority," but otherwise their only recourse is patient submission. "Whoever teaches the contrary is an Antichrist, liar, and deceiver.[10]

Marpeck calls the Protestant reformers the whore of Babylonian, Leviathan, Antichrists, so-called evangelicals, so-called Christians, and "no Christians." Such comments clearly locate Marpeck in a trajectory in which one might expect his theology to differ from his opponents, and it does. We observe that Marpeck aligns his theology and his church with the example of Christ, which in his eyes his opponents reject.

Concerning the Lowliness of Christ

A central component of Marpeck's theology is the humanity of Christ, which is a central feature of his 1547 letter *Concerning the Lowliness of Christ*, and makes visible his Anabaptist direction. The tract is a lengthy discussion of the function of the humanity—the humility—of Christ in the life of the church.

The treasure of the "gospel of Christ" is Christ himself. In Christ is hidden all that the Father, God, would reveal to us, and Christ reveals the Father in his "external teaching," that is bodily teaching.[11] It is this revelation in Christ that makes his humanity so important. It is in observing the earthly Jesus that believers learn of God and through the Holy Spirit are brought to know God inwardly. It is through the incarnation, the presence of God in Jesus Christ, that earthly creatures can become heavenly creatures.[12]

Marpeck likens the humanity of Christ to the ark of the covenant, a locked trunk in which the treasures of God are hidden. This ark was

---

9. Marpeck, "Exposé," 28–29.
10. Marpeck, "Exposé," 29.
11. Marpeck, *Writings of Pilgram Marpeck*, 429.
12. Marpeck, *Writings of Pilgram Marpeck*, 431.

destroyed on the cross and Jesus spent three days in hell. As his "physical suffering and death proclaimed the Word to men living in the body," so he brought salvation to those in the prison of hell. With the resurrection, the ark is destroyed and its contents revealed, death was overcome, including for all the saints from the Old Testament who had waited and hoped for the coming of Christ for their salvation.[13]

Salvation for sinners begins with the humility of Christ, that is, in his humanity. Through baptism, the believer identifies with the humility of Christ, and with Christ the believer dies to sin and is buried in his death. Then through resurrection with Christ, the believer rises to new life. The faithful then dwell with Christ in the risen temple of his body.[14]

Dwelling in the risen body of Christ, the church, is a climax in Marpeck's line of thought. Here, in this temple, God is apprehended, seen and heard. The church is thus an extension of the body of Christ, an extension of the incarnation in the world. Through participation in the church believers are united to God. Observing the gifts that come through the church as the body of Christ one knows God and can praise God. Equally important, with the gifts that God gives the church, its members serve one another and witness to the presence of Christ in the world.[15]

As high priest before God, Christ "accomplishes the priestly office in the hearts of the faithful." Thus the office and mission of Christ continues in the "earthen vessels" of the members of the church. Care must be taken to protect these vessels, and also to watch so that "our earthen vessel does not cause offense to anyone else." Further, God has endowed every single member for service to the church. "The gifts in every single member must be heard and seen," and no member escapes some endowment from "the treasures of Christ."[16]

That the church is the temple of the body of Christ means that the church works with the means of Christ. The church as a continuation of the incarnation brings rejection of the sword into the center of the conversation and makes it an intrinsic characteristic of the church. The disciples of Christ operate with the "patience of Christ."[17] Lack of patience means to trust in weapons, which is the opposite of trusting in Christ. Marpeck uses harsh

---

13. Marpeck, *Writings of Pilgram Marpeck*, 431–33.
14. Marpeck, *Writings of Pilgram Marpeck*, 434–36.
15. Marpeck, *Writings of Pilgram Marpeck*, 436.
16. Marpeck, *Writings of Pilgram Marpeck*, 440–42.
17. Marpeck, *Writings of Pilgram Marpeck*, 448.

language against those who claim to have "adopted the gospel" but then have accepted the patience of Christ only in appearance. They are "the Philistines [who] now send the ark back home again." They trust only human power.[18] True disciples have been called from "the horrible darkness of this world to His marvelous light," and those who follow the impatience of weapons are "false priests" and "so-called Christians."[19]

The reference to trusting in weapons visualizes specifically the Protestant forces of the Schmalkald war. At the time Marpeck writes, the Protestant forces of the Schmalkald League have been defeated by the Catholic forces of Emperor Charles V, and imperial forces occupy Augsburg where Marpeck lives. He seems particularly disturbed by the Protestants since they appeared initially to portray the gospel over against the papal church. These, however, are the "false priests" who are like "thieves who run ahead and lag behind Christ." They presume to teach those who are under God's judgment, but their building collapses and they perish. "They are destroyed by the human violence and protection under which they build their edifice," references to their defeat and the occupation of Augsburg by the forces of Charles V.[20]

Because of the works that they saw Jesus perform, the disciples confessed him as "the Lord Jesus Christ the true God, the Son of the Father." The Holy Spirit now prepares the way for the followers of Christ, who continue his presence in the world. As Christ's followers, their service consists of "external preaching, teaching, miracles, baptism, footwashing, the Lord's Supper, discipline, chastisement, and admonition."[21] These are all visible, external ceremonies and practices, which are extensions of Christ's ministry. Working within the believer, the Holy Spirit transforms these external ceremonies into the continuation of the body of Christ in the world.

To this point, most of the way through the tract, Marpeck has focused on the visible, human mission of Christ. A new element enters when he makes a trinitarian reference. Following the Western theological tradition, Marpeck states that the Holy Spirit "proceeds from the Father and the Son,"[22] and the Spirit "witnesses to the Father and Son in the hearts of

---

18. Marpeck, *Writings of Pilgram Marpeck*, 448.
19. Marpeck, *Writings of Pilgram Marpeck*, 450, 451, 452.
20. Marpeck, *Writings of Pilgram Marpeck*, 451–52.
21. Marpeck, *Writings of Pilgram Marpeck*, 453.
22. With the phrase "from the Father and the Son," Marpeck locates himself clearly on the side of the Western tradition in what is called the *filioque* controversy. The Western

the faithful."[23] The Spirit takes Christ's law from the Father and the Son and copies it into the hearts of believers, so that "the laws and new commandments of Christ the Lord are written by the finger of God."[24] Using language close to the variant reading of 1 John 5:7,[25] Marpeck writes that there are three witnesses, Father, Spirit and Word, to the invisible, heavenly being of God, and that they have also witnessed to people on earth "in visible, tangible, and bodily form."[26] Miracles of the Son revealed the Father, and "the Son taught the external words, which He Himself was as the Word of the Father, and revealed the Father," and was "glorified before man as true God." The dove at his baptism testified that God "was his Father." Marpeck brings these various witnesses together with a trinitarian statement: "Although God is, and remains, a Spirit in three persons, Father, Word, and Spirit, and is, eternally, invisible heavenly unity, nevertheless Father, Son, and Holy Spirit witnessed before men on earth in bodily, visible form . . . as one unitary Spirit, God, Father, and Son."[27] This statement does not pose trinitarian doctrine as a foundational statement. Rather it presupposes the prior emphasis on the earthly witness of Jesus, and references Trinity in order to underscore the prior emphasis.

Citing 1 John 5:8, Marpeck notes that the Spirit also witnesses with "water and blood" to Christ "as true man on earth." Believers are baptized "with the co-witness of the three names and persons, God the Father, Son, and Holy Spirit" in an "exact copy of Christ's command."[28] Along with these earthly and heavenly co-witnesses, the twelve apostles are also co-witnesses to Christ and to the liberty of Christ written in the heart by the Holy Spirit. This transitions to the witness of the Spirit in the church, since the apostles preserve the patience of Christ's body. This temple, Christ's body, was erected for "perpetual worship" served by "a royal priesthood that is not perishable or destructible, but remains forever." This is the church that Christ has preserved through the centuries, and is now in the charge of the people to whom

---

church came to insist that the Holy Spirit proceeds from the Father and the Son, in contrast to the Eastern church that asserts the Spirit is from the Father through the Son.

23. Marpeck, *Writings of Pilgram Marpeck*, 458.

24. Marpeck, *Writings of Pilgram Marpeck*, 459.

25. Marpeck's reading appears in the Froshauer Bibel (see Froschouer, Christoffel), and is given in a footnote in the English NRSV.

26. Marpeck, *Writings of Pilgram Marpeck*, 459.

27. Marpeck, *Writings of Pilgram Marpeck*, 460.

28. Marpeck, *Writings of Pilgram Marpeck*, 459–60.

Marpeck is writing. "It behooves all faithful believers to exercise the greatest care for this ark of the new covenant, and ensure that it may not be broken and seized by the enemy, and the treasures of Christ robbed."[29]

If one assumes the doctrine of the Trinity as an abstract, transcendent, intrinsically true given without need of validation, one can of course insert Marpeck's frequent references to Father, Son, Word, or Spirit into it and proclaim him classically or traditionally trinitarian, just like those whom he condemned as "not Christians," "Philistines," "false priests," and "so-called Christians." In this case, his rejection of the sword and his new ecclesiology become secondary to the important common theology he shares with his opponents.

On the other hand, a different picture emerges if we begin with the idea that Marpeck's new Anabaptist identity shapes the way he has come to understand theology. In this case, one observes his emphasis on the witness of the visible Christ on earth, which in turn makes rejection of the sword a primary or central aspect of his thought. In this case, his theology would reflect a commitment to build the church on the narrative of Jesus Christ. It is still true that Marpeck knows about and understands the traditional understanding of Trinity, but not as a standalone, unquestioned given, used as foundation piece. It serves rather to underscore his prior understanding of the importance of the earthly Jesus. Stated another way, his theologizing begins with and is specific to the biblical account of Jesus, not with the category of the Trinity. This conclusion is clear when one reads his tracts *Exposé of the Babylonian Whore* and *Lowliness of Christ* together.

With *Exposé* and *Concerning the Lowliness of Christ*, we followed the argument of two complete treatises. The conclusion about reading Marpeck's theology as Anabaptist rather than a version of classic orthodoxy also applies to comments when Marpeck was writing about his understandings of sacrament, Lord's Supper and baptism, and where he was either editing someone else's writing or engaging in a detailed discussion with a specific interlocutor.

The Admonition

Marpeck's *Admonition* of 1542 consists of a re-edition of Bernard Rothman's 1533 *Bekenntnis* or *Confession of Two Sacraments* with major additions by

---

29. Marpeck, *Writings of Pilgram Marpeck*, 460–61.

Marpeck. The major focus of *Admonition* is baptism and Lord's Supper. Two passages that Marpeck added have significance for the current discussion.

One passage comes in additions Marpeck made to a section of Rothman's tract on Paul's understanding of baptism. Marpeck uses language of Father, Son and Spirit to talk about the sign and the essence of a sacrament. He writes that "children born of the Spirit and nature of Christ" do that "which the Father, through the Spirit, performs in the inner man." That is, in baptism the external working, following the external (human) Christ is parallel to the inner working of the Father through the Spirit. And baptism is performed in the formulaic name of Father, the Son and Holy Spirit, "for the Son of Man cannot be without the Father and the Spirit, nor can the Spirit and the Father be without the Son of Man." In a comment directed against spiritualists such as Schwenckfeld, Marpeck's point is the external observances are necessary in order to have the inner working of the Spirit, and also that externals without the inner working of the Spirit are a denial of the Father and the Spirit.[30]

Later in *Admonition* Marpeck engages a discussion of the Holy Spirit and forgiveness. He writes that what he called the "ancient church," the people of God in the Old Testament, did not yet have the authority to forgive sins. That authority comes only with the gift of the Holy Spirit, which Christ conferred on the church only after his ascension, when he was seated at the right hand of the Father. It was then that the promised "Holy Spirit could build His temple and church in the hearts of the believers. Before that, the material, destructible temple of His body, as the figurative temple, was an entrance and preparation to the indestructible temple of His body, raised up in the resurrection and ascension to heaven, in Himself and in those whom He built up for the church." This church is the "temple of all believers and the Holy Spirit," and Christ is to be worshipped in this temple.[31]

In neither of these two passages from the *Admonition* does Marpeck refer explicitly to the Trinity nor use specifically trinitarian doctrine. However, he does use much biblical language of Father, Son, and Spirit. In particular, his language is close to John 5:19: "The Son can do nothing on his own, but only what he sees the Father doing; for whatever the

---

30. Marpeck, *Writings of Pilgram Marpeck*, 195–96, quotes 195. In addition to John Rempel's designation of this text as "sketching out the role of the Trinity" (Marpeck, *Later Writings*, 72, 74n9), Blough argues that these passages supply a "Trinitarian foundation" to Marpeck's argument. Blough, *Christ in Our Midst*, 108–9. The argument to follow provides a different analysis.

31. Marpeck, *Writings of Pilgram Marpeck*, 232.

Father does, the Son does likewise," and Eph 4:4–6: "There is one body and one Spirit, just as you were called to the one hope of your calling, one Lord, one faith, one baptism, one God and Father of all, who is above all and through all and in all." As I (Denny) learned long ago in seminary, recitation of the baptismal formula of Matt 28:19 and appearance of biblical language of God the Father, the Son and the Holy Spirit is not yet a doctrine of the Trinity. In that light, it seems that these passages from Marpeck might be better described as biblical, following the pattern described in *Concerning the Lowlines of Christ*.

The *Response*

Marpeck's *Response* of 578 pages was written in two parts from 1542 to 1546 in reply to Caspar Schwenckfeld's *Judgement*, which in return was written as a reply to Marpeck's *Admonition*.[32] The *Response* puts on display Marpeck's concentration with the humanity or human nature of Christ as the beginning point of his theology. His humanity gives visible, external reality to the working of God in the world. This visible, material aspect is accomplished by the Holy Spirit, which means that the working of Christ in and with the believer has both external and internal dimensions, which are inseparable. Apart from faith, it is possible to have the external function alone, but without the faith produced by the Spirit that external exercise is meaningless. With faith, however, it is the continuation of Christ in the world. Marpeck saw the church as the extension of the incarnation, made possible by the working of the Spirit in the life of the believers. Christ's human nature serves as the visible model for this working, and believers—the church—then continue it in the world.

In the seventy pages of John Rempel's abridged English translation from the *Response*, three passages refer specifically to the Trinity. After discussion of the spiritual nourishment that comes from feeding on the untransfigured body of Christ offered for our sins, Marpeck writes,

> Even now Christ is here according to the flesh and according to human nature; they have been taken up into God of very God, who is Spirit. Therefore, Christ's flesh is also God, as it is also the Holy Spirit, in the oneness of the Trinity, a lifegiving power yet without annulling his true humanity and flesh. His two natures,

---

32. Marpeck, *Later Writings*, 68, 72.

forms, and characteristics are united in one. This is how we may understand Paul's verse, . . . "the Lord is Spirit" (2 Cor 3).[33]

As was the case in *Concerning the Lowliness of Christ*, Marpeck appeals to the Trinity and trinitarian doctrine as a way to preserve his prior emphasis on the presence of the humanity of Christ to believers for salvation in spite of or along with the transfiguration of Christ by the Holy Spirit after his resurrection and ascension.

Some pages later Marpeck again mentions the Trinity as a way to preserve the two natures of Christ. He states that he agrees with Schwenckfeld that the incarnate Christ sits at the right hand of God in the Godhead. "Christ is God according to his humanity; his transfigured, divinized, and glorified flesh is to be adored." That is, the transfigured humanity of Christ is a part of the Godhead and thus part of the Trinity. But Marpeck's primary reason for referring to the Trinity is to assert that Christ's humanity and deity are one, undivided person. "We will not concern ourselves with the witness of the Holy Trinity except to confess one person of the Word and flesh."[34] For validation, Marpeck refers to the variant reading of 1 John 5:7–8 noted earlier: "There are three who give witness in heaven: the Father, the Word, and the Holy Spirit, and the three have one ministry." Marpeck calls these three the "Holy Trinity." His concern is to assert that a unified human and divine Christ are one in the Trinity. "The glorified and divinized flesh of Christ, ascended to heaven, is part of the Word. . . . Otherwise John would have to say, 'There are four who give witness in heaven: the Father, the Word, the flesh of Christ, and the Holy Spirit.' The human flesh of Christ is included in the Holy Trinity as part of a single Godhead, to be worshiped with the Word as God." And "the human flesh and blood and bone of Christ, as described, shares equality in the Holy Trinity in and with the Word." In this passage, Marpeck's concern is making visible the claim that Jesus as humanity and deity is nonetheless one unified person, as seen in the Trinity, and on the other hand, accounting for the human Jesus as fully God and representative of God. This discussion thus forms part of Marpeck's understanding that the human Jesus through the working of the Spirit brings believers into contact with God who is Spirit, and then to portray the church as the extension of this human Christ and thus an extension of the incarnation. "Therefore, all true believers become

---

33. Marpeck, *Later Writings*, 114–15.
34. Marpeck, "Response to Caspar Schwenckfeld," 129.

members of his body through the life-giving humanity of Christ through the anointing of the Holy Spirit."[35]

The third reference to Trinity in the translation of *Response* mentions baptism "in the name of the Holy Trinity,"[36] a formulaic reference to the baptismal formula.

As the only references to Trinity in the translated portion of the *Response*, these three passages align with the argument that Marpeck's thought is better described as primarily biblical, focused on the narrative of Jesus Christ, rather than being specifically orthodox trinitarian.

Marpeck's Theological Model: "Specific to Jesus"

The intent thus far has been to demonstrate that in his theologizing, Pilgram Marpeck did not simply repeat or stand on the received theological tradition. Rather, befitting his rejection of both Roman and Lutheran directions, in his articulation of theology he reflects his new Anabaptist commitment, which was based on the biblical narrative of Jesus Christ. In this chapter we have seen that commitment in his emphasis on the importance of the human or external Christ, in making the rejection of the sword integral to what it meant to be a following of Christ, and in his stress on a visible church modeled on Christ. Situating Marpeck in a new theological direction also accounts for the sharp language he used to describe opponents, particularly the Protestants from whom he first learned the gospel but who then turned to defending use of the sword and advocating rebellion against constituted authority. If Marpeck is characterized as one who sought to be orthodox, or who sought a mediating position between Catholics and Protestants, his sharp language does not align with such a stance.

Foregrounding Marpeck's distinct, Anabaptist convictions in his theology places a premium on novelty. Rather than seeing his references to the received or traditional terminology as evidence of his acceptance of traditional theology, his adaptation and sometimes subordination of it becomes evidence of creative thinking and a desire to revise or reshape these "borrowed" ideas into new configurations. Stated another way, putting Marpeck's Anabaptist convictions first shows his commitment to a primarily biblical approach which is specific to Jesus.

---

35. Marpeck, "Response to Caspar Schwenckfeld," 129.
36. Marpeck, "Response to Caspar Schwenckfeld," 140.

To be sure, Marpeck did not provide a fleshed out, comprehensive Anabaptist theology. What is visible in his writings are only indications of a new direction. This discussion of the theology and the theological method of Pilgram Marpeck presumes that in some way Marpeck is relevant for us, for the social and political life of the church today. The question becomes, what kind of model does the historical figure of Pilgram Marpeck pose for the twenty-first century?

Applying Marpeck

Whether a creed treated as a transcendent, unqualified given or an action or writing by a revered historical figure, we object to the idea that historical observations produce models to be lifted up and transported across the centuries, to be then incorporated today. In other words, historical description should not become prescriptive for theology or practice today. Our suggestion for Marpeck in particular and for Anabaptism in general is a different way of understanding the relationship of historical observation to the contemporary scene and the contemporary church.

We need to understand that we are living today in an ongoing historical stream, an ongoing account of what Marpeck called the "living cross and hand of Christ," which he said "does not stand immoveable in one place."[37] This "living cross" rather than the immoveable stance of a creedal tradition is the defining source for the ongoing stream of Anabaptist history in all its diversity of forms and expressions.[38] Marpeck constitutes one important figure in that stream, visible through a bit more than four hundred and fifty years of its history.

We learn a lot from studying that changing, ever-flowing stream, and it is important to us because it shows how and where we—Anabaptism or Anabaptisms—came into existence as an identifiable historical entity and attained our current status. But descriptions of segments of that stream ought not be lifted up and transported across the centuries and used to prescribe how we necessarily navigate the stream or live in the story today. Instead, as was Marpeck, we are more interested in the "living cross," which he described as the "way from which truth comes" and "the truth from which life comes."[39] We stand in a stream of Christian and Anabaptist

---

37. Marpeck, "Exposé," 29.
38. See Mast and Weaver, *Defenseless Christianity*, esp. 28–31, 78–80.
39. Marpeck, "Exposé," 29.

history that has shaped us but our answers and outlook today are not necessarily prescribed by descriptions of segments of that historical stream, whether fourth or fifth or twelfth or sixteenth centuries.

The specific thing we learn from Marpeck is to keep focused on the Jesus of the Christian story. It is in Jesus' human life that we see the presence and the character of God in the world. Being rooted in this story—Jesus' story—is a stance to the world. "It is a way to live in the world—a posture—shaped by the powerful story of Jesus Christ."[40] Of necessity it must be described as a stance or a posture—the world changes and thus we are always in a process of asking again in the new situation how the narrative of Jesus should shape our understandings and our actions.[41] This process requires continually retrieving the story of Jesus to apply that story to our current walk in the stream of Anabaptist history. What we learn from Marpeck most specifically is a direction to travel in this ongoing story, and we follow the direction that Marpeck points because we are Christians. That is, we are people whose primary identity comes from the narrative of Jesus. Marpeck is one historical person who reminds us who we are as Christians, and who points out some important issues missed by the majority of people who call themselves Christians.

Marpeck makes these theological moves in ways that are compatible with the mainstream trinitarian tradition. But for Marpeck, the mainstream trinitarian tradition is not posited as the necessary given, assumed outline to be filled in. Rather, Marpeck writes first of all as an Anabaptist, seeking to develop theology that assumes discipleship to the Jesus of the gospel narratives. That approach is visible in his *Exposé* that challenges the Lutherans' use of the sword but does not mention Trinity. It is visible in the development of thought throughout his letter, *Concerning the Lowliness of Christ*, which has extensive discussion about applying the humanity of Christ, and then near the end appeals to trinitarian doctrine to further underscore the importance of the humanity of Christ.[42]

---

40. Mast and Weaver, *Defenseless Christianity*, 79.

41. Mast and Weaver, *Defenseless Christianity*, 80.

42. See Appendix B, which shows that Marpeck is not alone among Anabaptists in his preference for precise biblical rather than technically trinitarian language.

Conclusion

Marpeck emerges from this analysis as an assertive Anabaptist who displays theology that reflects his choice to cast his churchly lot with the dissident Anabaptist movement. The model he provides us is not a model to be specifically emulated but his model does point us to the "living cross" or the stance that is "specific to Jesus" which does show the way. It seems clear that Marpeck's theology does indicate a direction new for his time, a direction based in and shaped by Jesus as the nonviolent Word of God. Christians today who are shaped by the Anabaptist tradition continue in that direction, a direction whose implications we are still discovering. The idea that we are in a process of continually reaching back to Jesus keeps front and center the fact that the good news about Jesus Christ as nonviolent Word of God is never fully contained in any one particular formula or statement and that this good news always has the potential to disturb contemporary culture.

CHAPTER 3

The Word of God in Menno's Christology

We teach and believe, and this is the thrust of the whole Scriptures, that the whole Christ is from head to foot, both inside and outside, visible and invisible, God's first-born and only begotten Son; the incomprehensible eternal Word, by whom all things were created, the first-born of every creature. —Menno Simons[1]

The Word of God and the Scandal of Dutch Mennonite Christology

MENNO SIMONS AND THE Dutch Anabaptists offered a distinct vision of the Word of God as an incorruptible seed from which Jesus Christ was conceived and through which the ecclesial body of Christ now regenerates the lives of believers who become attached to Christ's body in baptism. This controversial view—sometimes known as "celestial flesh Christology"—offers another illustration of how early Anabaptist theologizing explained the Word of God as a disruptive and transformative force apart from its presentation in Scripture—while of course consistent with that presentation in the Bible.

The argument that Jesus received his flesh—and therefore his humanity—not from his mother Mary but from heaven, has long been a source of conflict and embarrassment for Mennonite piety and historical theology. This view, with precedent in the second-century gnostic teachings of Valentinus and Marcion, and appearing again among such "heretical" sects as the Cathars and Bogomiles, was taken up in the sixteenth century by Radical Reformation leaders such as Caspar Schwenckfeld

---

1. Menno, *Complete Writings*, 335–36. This chapter is a revised and differently framed version of an earlier article, Mast, "Jesus' Flesh," 173–90.

and Melchior Hoffman, both of whom no doubt contributed to the long shadow of celestial flesh Christology among Dutch Anabaptists.[2] Not long after Menno joined the Dutch Anabaptist movement in 1536, following the violent apocalypse at Münster, he was wracked by doubt and anxiety regarding the celestial flesh teaching of the Dutch Anabaptist brotherhood, becoming convinced of the truth of this doctrine only after lengthy discussion, many days of fasting, and months of biblical study. Although it was not his preferred doctrinal topic, a large amount of his published writing ended up being devoted to defending celestial flesh Christology to Calvinist detractors like John a Lasco and Martin Micron. For such Reformed church leaders, celestial flesh Christology was a basis for rejecting the validity of Mennonite doctrine, a rejection that appeared again and again in Reformed (and Lutheran) confessions.

At the same time, celestial flesh Christology was a basis for division among Mennonite groups. Anabaptist communities in Upper Germany that had been in fellowship with Dutch Mennonite groups refused in 1559 to accept either strict shunning or the celestial flesh Christology of the conservative Dutch groups as confessional requirements for their congregations, thus leading Dirk Philips and other Dutch Mennonite leaders to ban the Upper Germans. This, in turn, caused more tolerant Dutch Anabaptist groups who rejected this decision to leave the main body of Mennonites in the Netherlands; these more tolerant congregations became known as the Waterlanders—after the place of origin for a significant number of the dissenters.

The question of the nature of Jesus' flesh was to play a significant role in contentious discussions throughout the seventeenth century among Dutch Mennonite communities who sought to achieve confessional unity amid multiple and repeated divisions. Confessions of faith written by Dutch Mennonites to achieve unity at different times and contexts featured celestial flesh Christology—at times emphasizing and at other times de-emphasizing the doctrine. Compilers of Mennonite martyrologies in the seventeenth century edited their collections to either highlight or downplay the adherence of Anabaptist martyrs to the heavenly flesh of Jesus, sometimes producing vituperative exchanges between such editors.[3] Modern editors of the writings of Menno Simons have sometimes flinched at the extended discussions and debates about the incarnation found in

2. Krahn, "Incarnation of Christ," 19.
3. Sprunger, "Dutch Anabaptists and the Telling," 170–73.

Menno's work. In John Funk's 1871 English edition, Menno's *Very Plain and Discreet Answer to Martin Micron* is abridged significantly because, according to the publisher, "in the translation of the writings of Menno Simons upon the 'Incarnation of Christ'" there were parts that were considered "of no importance in the illustration and explanation of the subject," and "were not edifying to the reader."[4] These parts, it turns out, were almost invariably instances of Menno's discussion of Mary's menstrual flux (*menftrual bloet*), where Jesus' seed was said to have coagulated, and which Menno argued was the extent of Mary's contribution to Jesus' bodily origin.[5] These references to Menno's mistaken understanding that women contribute nothing to the formation of the human embryo were included in the 1956 translation by Leonard Verduin, but with an introduction by J. C. Wenger in which he labeled Menno's treatment of the issue as "tedious and tiresome" and wished that Menno "would have had more good sense than to waddle through the mire."[6] Wenger urges the reader to avoid reading the majority of the *Reply to Micron*, identifying section X as "the only edifying section in the entire *Reply*."[7]

More recent retrievals of Menno's theological convictions have also expressed discomfort about his view of the incarnation. Abraham Friesen's otherwise instructive book on the role of Erasmus' interpretation of the Great Commission in Anabaptist baptismal polemics assumes that Menno held to celestial flesh almost entirely as a pragmatic concession to Dutch Anabaptist conventions—an assumption that seems unlikely given Menno's stubborn refusal to be conformist in practically every other issue he confronted, either inside or outside the brotherhood.[8] More recently, Tom Finger has described Menno's "tedious" advocacy of "heavenly flesh Christology" as a conviction he held "most embarrassingly for Mennonites today."[9]

A few years ago, I (Gerald) received an e-mail from a member of the Christian Reformed Church who was studying article 18 of the Belgic Confession, which opposes "the heresy of the Anabaptists, who deny that Christ assumed human flesh of his mother."[10] This correspondent asked me whether

---

4. Menno, *Complete Writings*, 452.
5. Menno, *Opera omnia theologica*, 546–48.
6. Menno, *Complete Writings*, 436–37.
7. Menno, *Complete Writings*, 837.
8. Friesen, *Erasmus, the Anabaptists*, 62–64.
9. Finger, "Confessions of Faith," 283.
10. Schaff, *Evangelical Protestant Creeds*, 403.

Mennonites still denied that Christ received his flesh from Mary. His hope was that if Mennonites no longer made such a denial, perhaps the Belgic Confession could be revised to reflect this development. I, of course, responded that this view was peculiar to the Dutch Mennonites, that it had pretty much died out by the eighteenth century, and that no Mennonite group today that I knew of denied that Christ received his flesh from Mary.

That I would need to reassure an ecumenical partner today about Mennonite christological beliefs illustrates the long-standing significance of Menno's stubborn adherence to celestial flesh Christology. Perhaps the time has come not to simply reassure ourselves and others that Mennonite Christology today is orthodox but to reexamine again what Menno taught in order to see if there is anything we might learn from this strange conviction from a different time and place.

Menno's Understanding of Jesus' Flesh

In this chapter we investigate the possibility that Menno's christology was a valid theological effort to recover the heavenly power of the earthly Jesus to save us from our sins, from which we could learn today, and which confirms a particular Anabaptist understanding of the Word of God as the creative and transformative work of Jesus Christ. This reading of Menno's views on the incarnation have been shaped significantly by William Keeney, whose extensive and, in our view, definitive exploration of the grammar of Menno's Christology has proven Menno's thoroughgoing, if militant, Christian humanism.

According to Keeney, Menno was convinced that Jesus became flesh in Mary without receiving his flesh from her.[11] Menno argues that although Jesus was born out of (*uit*) Mary he was not born from (*van*) Mary, but rather from (*van*) God.[12] This distinction was crucial for Menno because he assumed that had Jesus been born from Mary he would also have received corrupted flesh from her and would thus have been unable to be the bearer of human salvation.[13] Menno supported his view of Jesus' origin by invoking the Aristotelian theory of human conception whereby only the male

---

11. Keeney, *Development of Dutch Anabaptist Thought*, 89–100.

12. Keeney, *Development of Dutch Anabaptist Thought*, 91. An example of this argument is Menno's answer to the fifth objection in his "Een korte ende klare belydinge," in Menno, *Opera omnia theologica*, 531.

13. Keeney, *Development of Dutch Anabaptist Thought*, 92.

seed contributes substance to the embryo, while the female body provides nourishment and birth.[14] Keeney points out that the Aristotelian view was widely held in the centuries leading up to the time of Menno, including by Thomas Aquinas and Hilary of Poitiers, although Thomas did not apply this view to the incarnation as did both Hilary and Menno.[15]

Thomas, however, was concerned like Menno for the integrity and unity of Jesus as the incarnate Word even if he developed a different although somewhat parallel solution to the problem of how Jesus could be both divine and human without either one of these attributes simply being added to the other. According to Rowan Williams, Thomas emphasized that the Word who became flesh is not a general or abstract combination of two qualities but rather the "second person of the eternal Trinity" being given or expressed as Jesus Christ in human history. On this account, we cannot "adequately identify the divine Word without speaking of Jesus of Nazareth" while at the same time this historical human person Jesus of Nazareth is entirely an enactment and a communication of the divine Word and not in any way independent of the Word.[16] Thomas, in other words, comes close to the idea advocated by Menno that Jesus Christ is entirely a conception of the Word of God, whose flesh and spirit are united in their heavenly origin.

While Menno did not believe that Jesus received his flesh from Mary, he did assume that Jesus' flesh was human, although the humanity of Jesus' flesh was derived from the same substance as that of Adam's nature before the fall.[17] Menno therefore did not assume the inherently evil nature of human flesh, but rather the fallen nature of postlapsarian human flesh. He is thus distinguished from the gnostic writers mentioned earlier who assumed that flesh, like matter itself, was intrinsically evil.[18]

Furthermore, it is not the case that Menno exhibited hostility to women by assuming that Jesus could not have been conceived by Mary. For Menno,

---

14. Keeney, *Development of Dutch Anabaptist Thought*, 92.

15. Keeney, *Development of Dutch Anabaptist Thought*, 92. See also Irwin, "Embryology and Incarnation," 94–95.

16. Williams, *Christ the Heart*, 29–31.

17. Keeney, *Development of Dutch Anabaptist Thought*, 97.

18. Burkhart's study of Menno's views on the incarnation concludes that Menno believed that "all flesh is inherently evil," a claim that Burkhart later retracted in a correction where he stated unequivocally that "Menno did not teach that the flesh of man is inherently evil." See Burkhart, "Note: Menno Simons on the Incarnation," 122–23, Burkhart, "Menno Simons on the Incarnation (Continued)," 179.

the problem with Mary is not that she was a woman, but that she was a fallen human being.[19] His appropriation of the Aristotelian view of male-originated conception was an incidental argument used to support his more basic conviction that Jesus' flesh came from God, not from fallen humanity. Moreover, Menno did not believe, like Valentinus, that Jesus passed through Mary like water through a pipe. Rather, Jesus "was fed and nourished in truly human fashion in her virgin body by ordinary food and drink."[20] Jesus received this nourishment, in the Aristotelian theory accepted by Menno, through Mary's menstrual blood or flux.[21] Menno's extensive discussion of the role of menstrual blood in the process of birth suggests that he is less squeamish than some of his descendants in considering the role of women's bodies in procreation—even if he was mistaken about the particulars.

In his debate with Martin Micron, Menno also rejected the view that the sinful nature of humanity "comes from the marital intimacy that was given in God's original creation."[22] Instead, Menno insisted that sin originated in Adam's transgression. This offers further evidence that Menno was not somehow hostile to bodies and human biology. Rather, he sought to offer access to the redemption of the body through association with Christ's body, a body that was fully free from the constraints of human sin and could therefore be the agent of human liberation—"the spiritual brazen serpent" and the "true bread from heaven, which is not made of natural grain or wheat (I mean of our sinful flesh) but comes of the dew of the eternal Word and is the only true food for our souls, by which we shall live forever, if we eat of Him through true faith."[23]

Thus, for Menno, Christ was both divine and human insofar as he was wholly of God, undivided in his nature, "a single person, God's own firstborn Son and only begotten Son," consisting of "holy and saving flesh."[24] It is precisely since Christ was fully God that his willingness to become a servant

---

19. For a discussion of celestial flesh that places this conviction in the context of contemporary feminist understandings of the body, see Biesecker-Mast, "Spiritual Knowledge," 213.

20. Menno, *Complete Writings*, 794.

21. Menno, *Complete Writings*, 850; Irwin, "Embryology and Incarnation," 95–96.

22. Menno, *Complete Writing*, 851.

23. Menno, *Complete Writings*, 820–21.

24. Menno, *Complete Writings*, 793, 820.

had meaning, that his ability to minister to humans became visible, and that his obedience unto death was in fact an offering on our behalf.[25]

To fully grasp what was at stake here in Menno's argument it will be helpful to rehearse the rhetorical situation to which Menno was responding. Menno's texts concerning the incarnation were written in the context of debates with two Reformed church leaders—John a Lasco (the superintendent of the Reformed state church in East Friesland) and Martin Micron (an influential Reformed minister from Norden in East Friesland).[26] In both cases, Menno was engaging in public debates with the church party that had come into ascendancy in northwest Germany. Menno clearly recognized greater kinship with these Reformed leaders than with the Catholic regime that had put a price on his head in Holland. He initially addressed both John a Lasco and Martin Micron (and their people) as brothers and friends.

The first debate with John a Lasco in 1544 was an occasion when a Lasco sought to test how dangerous Menno's views were and also to convince him to accept the Reformed perspective. No doubt Menno hoped to prove the validity of Anabaptist faith and perhaps to achieve some tolerance by the Reformed regime, without compromising his community's convictions and practices. The discussion with a Lasco ranged over such topics as baptism, original sin, justification, the calling of ministers, and the incarnation, with the latter topic prompting a Lasco to ask Menno for a written confession of his views on the incarnation.[27]

When Menno provided the written text for a Lasco, he then published it without Menno's consent and subsequently attacked it in a treatise published in 1545, the same year that Countess Anna of Oldenburg, acting under the influence of a Lasco, decreed that Menno and his people be required to leave the country, while the more threatening Anabaptists, including those associated with the terrorist cells of Jan van Batenburg and the spiritualist conventicles of David Joris were to be executed. Menno's second book on the incarnation (1554) was published nine years later in response to a Lasco's attack. In the preface to the 1554 response to a Lasco, Menno no longer evinces much hope that his argument will win any tolerance from Reformed authorities: "I know very well that my truth will probably remain a falsehood in the eyes of the learned ones"[28]

25. Menno, *Complete Writings*, 814–15.
26. Menno, *Complete Writings*, 19–25.
27. Krahn, "Menno Simons," 580.
28. Menno, *Complete Writings*, 785.

Menno's motivations instead lie with "pure love for my Lord and Saviour and for his holy Word and out of love for my dear brethren" as well as "a kindly feeling which I entertain toward my opponent."[29]

The year before he published his response to John a Lasco, the events which led to Menno's debate with Martin Micron had begun to unfold. Zwinglian refugees from London had come to Wismar, where Menno and his followers offered them assistance. In the course of their fraternization, the Mennonites and the Zwinglians got into a doctrinal dispute that led to a formal public debate, with Martin Micron coming from Norden to assist the Zwinglians. The first day of debate was an uninterrupted eleven hour discussion of the same issues Menno had earlier debated with a Lasco concluding with a common meal. The topic of the incarnation was reserved for a separate occasion, nine days later on February 15, 1554. The discussion about the incarnation clearly exceeded the bounds of civility and led both to the public revelation of Menno's hiding place (which the Reformed party had promised to keep secret) and to Micron's publication of his account of the disputation two years later. Menno responded four months later with his *Reply to Martin Micron*, followed shortly with his *Epistle to Martin Micron*, the first of which dealt almost exclusively with the debate on the incarnation.[30]

One obvious dimension of the rhetorical situation then was a doctrinal conflict in which Menno was taking up the weaker position, first of all in the sense that it was held by a religious minority against the confessional regime that sought to enforce the more "orthodox" position on the incarnation—that Jesus was born from, and not merely out of, Mary. In the case of John a Lasco, the initial discussion had led to a decree of exile against the Mennonites. In the case of the dispute with Micron, which had begun with an offering by the Mennonites of material assistance and relief to beleaguered Zwinglians, the result was that Menno's hiding place was divulged and a leading Reformed minister had published another book against him. But a second aspect of the "weaker argument" taken up by Menno was that he was challenging the long-standing orthodox formulation dating back to the council of Chalcedon that Jesus had two natures: one derived from his earthly mother and the other from God. Micron's inflection of this Chalcedonian understanding apparently accepted that Jesus contained within

---

29. Menno, *Complete Writings*, 785.
30. Menno, *Complete Writings*, 836.

himself two persons—one the son of God and the other the son of Mary.[31] Against this division, Menno insisted, perhaps with some excessive redundancy, on an "undivided Christ."[32]

Yet, this seemingly redundant insistence is understandable when we recognize the apparent link for Menno at this point, felt by him in a quite material way, between Reformed soteriology and Chalcedonian Christology. For Menno, the two natures or persons in Christ assumed by the Reformed were of a piece with the incongruence between the confession and practice he observed among the Reformed. How could those who claimed Christ as their salvation persecute other Christians with violence, or even use the sword of the magistrate to execute unbelievers? Writing to Micron as a follow-up to his refutation of Micron's account of their disputation, Menno asks: "If you had tasted the sweet Word of God and the fruits of the world to be, you would never afflict the pious as you have done by your untrue, false writing, nor would you encourage any of their bloody doings, but point them to the meek Lamb, and let the dead bury the dead."[33] Moreover, Menno writes, the sword of the magistrate cannot be used by Christians to kill anyone, even wrongdoers: "For he who is a Christian must follow the Spirit, Word, and example of Christ, no matter whether he be emperor, king, or whatever he be."[34] In this respect Menno eloquently recalls his response to Micron during their earlier debate, in a passage that is worth quoting at length:

> When you proposed your pharisaical, Herod-like question concerning the magistracy, I said nothing more to you than that it would hardly become a Christian ruler to shed blood. For this reason, if the transgressor should truly repent before his God and be reborn of Him, he would then also be a chosen saint and child of God, a fellow partaker of grace, a spiritual member of the Lord's body, sprinkled with His precious blood and anointed with His Holy Ghost, a living grain of the Bread of Christ and an heir to eternal life; and for such an one to be hanged on the gallows, put on the wheel, placed on the stake, or in any manner be hurt in body or goods by another Christian, who is of one heart, spirit, and soul with him, would look somewhat strange and unbecoming in the light of the compassionate, merciful, kind nature, disposition,

---

31. Menno, *Complete Writings*, 334–35.
32. Menno, *Complete Writings*, 865–84.
33. Menno, *Complete Writings*, 922.
34. Menno, *Complete Writings*, 922.

spirit, and example of Christ, the meek Lamb—which example He has commanded all His chosen children to follow.[35]

This passage exhibits most vividly the social understanding of salvation assumed by Menno. For those who are members of Christ, every one is a potential brother or sister, and thus is to be treated as such. In his confession about the incarnation written for John a Lasco, Menno had acknowledged that the peace brought by Christ has an inward dimension. But, he insisted, "whoever has this inward, Christian peace in his heart will never more be found guilty before God and this world of turmoil, treason, mutiny, murder, theft," but rather such people "follow peace with all men."[36] This was the basis for Menno's understanding of "true evangelical faith," that it could not "lie dormant" but would "manifest itself in all righteousness and works of love."[37]

Such inward and social peace is rooted for Menno in the regenerative power of the work of Jesus Christ; that is, the creative and intrinsically nonviolent power of the Word of God. Menno asks, "For how could true brethren and sisters of Jesus Christ, the well-disposed children of God, who with Christ Jesus are born of God the Father and the powerful seed of the divine Word in Christ Jesus, who are regenerated by Christ, partake of His Spirit and nature, who have been made like unto Him, are Christian and heavenly-minded—how can such people teach or stage turmoil of any kind?"[38]

It seems clear that one way Menno imagined Christians could justify killing is to accept a divided Christ, a Christ in whom both sin and salvation coexist. Egil Grislis defends Menno's critique of Chalcedonian Christology on precisely this point: "He (Menno) cannot be blamed for all-too-readily connecting the Chalcedonian two-nature Christology, with a doctrine of justification which all too readily admitted sin into Christian existence—and then went on to persecute, torture, and to kill."[39] Indeed, Grislis suggests, "for Menno in his time and circumstances, it was a monophysite Christology that insured the possession of truth and salvation."[40]

Grislis makes clear what was at stake for Menno in his commitment to an "undivided Jesus." The main issue has to do with what is meant by

35. Menno, *Complete Writings*, 920.
36. Menno, *Complete Writings*, 423.
37. Menno, *Complete Writings*, 307.
38. Menno, *Complete Writings*, 423.
39. Grislis, "Doctrine of the Incarnation," 30.
40. Grislis, "Doctrine of the Incarnation," 30.

salvation. Is salvation merely a forensic event, an adjustment of our standing or status before God? Or does salvation involve practical empowerment toward liberation from sin? Menno was concerned that the orthodox or Reformed insistence that Jesus' flesh came from earthly humanity simply reinforced the intractability of sin and a weak forensic view of salvation—cheap grace. By way of contrast, Menno believed that Jesus' holy humanity, his divine flesh, offered leverage against the corruption of the fall and freed Christians to share in Christ's divinity, to become themselves whole human beings once more, no longer divided within themselves or against others. As William Keeney succinctly restates this view, "The Incarnation through the new creature in Christ offers the ontological basis for real obedience."[41]

Thus, from the perspective of Menno, the same incorruptible seed from which Christ was conceived, through which the Word became flesh and dwelt among us, will also produce fruit in the lives of those who have become members of Christ's incorruptible body. Through the power of the Word of God, our flesh, too, can become divine.

Menno's Understanding of the Church's Seed

The process by which human beings can be regenerated by the "undivided Christ" necessarily involves the church—the body of Christ. Menno believed that the church had inherited from Jesus Christ the incorruptible seed that had birthed his body—both the historical Jesus and the historical church. "By faith," Menno wrote in his *Foundation of Christian Doctrine*, human beings "become new creatures, born of God and transplanted from Adam in Christ."[42] Menno makes this observation in the context of his discussion of the Lord's Supper, an event he considered a memorial meal on the one hand, but also an occasion where when the meal is rightly celebrated with "faith, love, attentiveness, peace, unity of heart and mind, there Jesus Christ is present with His grace, Spirit, and promise."[43] In his discussion of the Lord's Supper Menno critiques the practice of including unrepentant sinners in the Lord's Supper because such a performance precisely contradicts the reality of Christ's incorruptible body as the basis for the church. Those who are joined to Christ are necessarily freed from sin, becoming "flesh of his flesh and bone of his bone, a true partaker of the body and

---

41. Keeney, "Incarnation," 64.
42. Menno, *Complete Writings*, 146.
43. Menno, *Complete Writings*, 148.

the blood of Christ."⁴⁴ A Lord's Supper which does not make visible such a liberating participation with Christ is false.

In Menno's writing, the process of regeneration seems to precede chronologically the constitution of the church. At the same time, the existence of the church in his writings is not divided logically from the new creature that is born into Christ. As Sjouke Voolstra puts it, "For Menno Simons, incarnation is the residence of Christ in the hearts of believers and the transformation of individuals who were not obedient to God into a people subject to God in obedience."⁴⁵

There is quite clearly for Menno a specific existential choice by human individuals to accept the work of Christ. This is not primarily an intellectual decision, an acknowledgment of Christ, or a matter of belief, but rather a shift in orientation, an embrace of the Word of God, and being joined to Christ: "In your life you must become so converted and changed that you become new creatures in Christ, that Christ be in you and you in Christ."⁴⁶ This process of conversion and reorientation involves the reception of the incorruptible seed, according to Menno: "Those who with Adam truly receive the promised Seed and are renewed and comforted in God, who are born from above by this same Seed, who are changed and converted from the disobedient nature of Adam to the obedient nature of the Word, Christ Jesus: these He calls flesh of his flesh and bone of His bone."⁴⁷

The incorruptible seed from which new believers are born is the basis for a change in orientation and identification. Being born from such seed immediately places one into relationship with others who have also been reborn in Christ and joined to one another in Christ. In Menno's book on *Christian Baptism* he makes explicit that the spiritual seed from which Christians are born is the seed of the "holy, Christian church." This is an "assembly of the righteous, and a community of saints; which church is begotten of God, of the living seed of the divine Word, and not of the teachings, institutions, and fictions of man."⁴⁸

The role of human choice in the reception of this "spiritual seed" is clear in Menno's book on baptism. Fallen children of Adam have the capacity, once they have reached an age of understanding, to respond to the

44. Menno, *Complete Writings*, 151.
45. Voolstra, *Menno Simons*, 66.
46. Menno, *Complete Writings*, 172, 96–97.
47. Menno, *Complete Writings*, 439.
48. Menno, *Complete Writings*, 234.

divine Word in faith and obedience, to repent of their sins and to accept baptism, in which, according to Menno they receive "remission of sins."[49] Yet, it is clear that salvation is the result of the work of Christ, not of a choice to accept this work and to embrace it. According to Menno, believers receive remission of sins, "not through baptism but in baptism" (*niet door den Doopfel maer in den Doopfel*) a distinction of prepositions that recalls Menno's claim that Jesus was born not from Mary but out of Mary.[50] Furthermore, while in baptism believers receive remission of sins, they are not "cleansed in baptism of our inherited sinful nature which is in our flesh, so that it is entirely destroyed in us, for it remains with us after baptism."[51] Menno, in other words, is not arguing for Christian perfectionism. Rather, he writes that because of God's gift of faith through God's Word, "we declare in the baptism (*in den doopfel*) we receive that we desire to die unto the inherent, sinful nature, and destroy it, so that it will no longer be master over our mortal bodies, even though such true believers are often overcome by sin."[52] For Menno, the capacity of humans to desire freedom from sin, a desire which is unleashed by the gift of God's enfleshed Word, is the condition of possibility for regeneration in baptism.

Elsewhere, in his *Reply to False Accusations*, Menno elaborates on the relationship between the remaining sinful nature and the freedom from that nature experienced by believers in baptism. He distinguishes between willful disobedience and actions resulting from "remnants of the old nature," the latter of which he describes as "human frailties, errors, and stumblings which are still found daily among saints and regenerate ones."[53] Although the willful disobedience of unbelievers and the lapses of conduct by regenerated believers both result from the same corrupt sinful nature, the difference is that believers "fight daily with their weak flesh in the Spirit and faith" whereas unbelievers "commit sin with relish and boldness."[54] Believers are acting, in other words, according to the new nature that they have received in opposition to the "remnants of the old nature" that remain. The "new nature" produces "evangelical fruit" such as "mercy, friendship, chastity, temperance,

---

49. Menno, *Complete Writings*, 244.
50. Menno, *Opera omnia theologica*, 406.
51. Menno, *Complete Writings*, 245.
52. Menno, *Complete Writings*, 245; Menno, *Opera omnia theologica*, 406. Menno adds that "we are not cleansed by the washing of the water, but by the Word of the Lord."
53. Menno, *Complete Writings*, 564–65.
54. Menno, *Complete Writings*, 564.

humility, confidence, truth, peace, and joy in the Holy Ghost," in spite of the "old nature."[55] The basic orientation is away from sin and toward the "doctrine, ceremonies, commands, prohibitions, and perfect example of Christ," rather than toward sin and away from Christ.[56]

For Menno, the capacity of believers to bear evangelical fruit, to live according to Christ, and to manifest "righteousness and works of love" is the result of the gift of the incarnation—the Word becoming flesh in Mary—a "single undivided person, Son and Christ, God's true and natural Son as to origin and essence, and Mary's supernatural Son as to His conception."[57] The same Word through which Adam and Eve were created has "by His almighty power raised them up again out of pure grace and love."[58] All who "firmly believe this wondrously high work . . . overcome the world; they are in God and God is in them." They "fear God, bury their sins, and turn from evil."[59] They are born of "the incorruptible seed of the holy divine Word" and will thus assist their brothers and sisters "in an evangelical manner, risk and give their lives for them in time of need."[60] Menno clarifies here that an "evangelical manner" means not with "swords and muskets" but after the example of Christ, "who for our sakes did not spare himself, but willingly yielded His life, that we through Him might live."[61]

Sjouke Voolstra has commented that in celestial flesh Christology, Anabaptists like Menno witnessed to the fact that in Christ "something entirely new has entered the world," a thing so original that "it cannot be part of the fallen creation nor can it be understood within human, philosophical categories."[62] This seemingly incomprehensible newness "does not make it less real," however. According to Voolstra, "It is the only reality which makes of the visible reality a sham and manifests itself provisionally in the disarmed community."[63] This new reality, revealed now in the faithful church, is the basis for a renewed perspective on the world and a new experience of self and other, for those who are joined to Christ's body in the

55. Menno, *Complete Writings*, 342–43.
56. Menno, *Complete Writings*, 343.
57. Menno, *Complete Writings*, 307, 884.
58. Menno, *Complete Writings*, 884.
59. Menno, *Complete Writings*, 885.
60. Menno, *Complete Writings*, 347.
61. Menno, *Complete Writings*, 347–48.
62. Voolstra, *Het Woord Is vlees geworden*, 213.
63. Voolstra, *Het Woord Is vlees geworden*, 213.

church. The church, as we will see below, is the place where we are saved, even if it is not the instrument of our salvation.

How Our Salvation Takes Place in the Church but Not Through It

Egil Grislis writes that "since Christology and soteriology are correlatives, a presently perceived flaw in one will necessarily lead the community of the faithful to question and rewrite the other." In Menno's time, the perception of his fellowship that prominent forms of Christianity did not manifest the evidences of salvation led Dutch Anabaptists to propose a rethinking of Chalcedonian Christology. That rethinking emphasized the power of God through the work of Jesus Christ to transform human beings, down to their very bodily knowledge and experience.

The question of whether Christianity really makes a difference is still with us today. In a recent book, Ron Sider has called attention to *The Scandal of the Evangelical Conscience.* Citing numerous statistics from US polling firms such as Gallop and Barna, Sider concludes that evangelical Christians are living lives no different from and in some cases worse than their "unsaved" neighbors, particularly when it comes to how they spend their money, their fidelity in marriage, and the commitment to racial equality and reconciliation.[64] By such evidences, evangelical Christians commit "treason," according to Sider. "With their mouths they claim that Jesus is Lord, but with their actions they demonstrate allegiance to money, sex, and self-fulfillment."[65] From this perspective it is not surprising that American evangelical Christians can enthusiastically support a political leader whose practices and policies contradict the way of Jesus Christ in nearly every respect—as large numbers of them did during the 2016 election—sometimes explicitly claiming support from a form of two-kingdom theology.

Sider recognizes that a significant cause of such "treason" is the "cheap grace" preached in many evangelical churches, along with an overemphasis on substitutionary atonement and justification at the expense of the Lordship of Christ and sanctification.[66] He argues for recovering the social aspect of salvation along with the personal aspect.[67] What is absent

---

64. Sider, *Scandal*, 17–29.
65. Sider, *Scandal*, 12–13.
66. Sider, *Scandal*, 55–69.
67. Sider, *Scandal*, 72–83.

from his framework is a meaningful consideration of how the personal and social aspect of salvation can be joined in a way that makes it impossible to recognize them separately. Menno's understanding of Jesus' holy flesh as accessible through the incorruptible seed in the church—provides just such a wholistic theology of the undivided Word of God—an undivided Christ, an undivided salvation, an undivided humanity. This undivided Christ preached by Menno challenges dualistic two-kingdom theology that grants legitimacy to violence for the sake of order. Not surprisingly, when Menno speaks of two kingdoms, they are opposed to one another in every way: one is connected with the prince of peace and the other with the prince of strife.[68] Thus Menno affirms the possibility of Christian political leadership but insists that a Christian magistrate could never wield the sword of execution against a human being for whom Christ died and who is therefore a potential brother or sister in Christ.[69] Because the Word of God is undivided, there is no place in Menno's theology for legitimating lethal violence, even violence wielded by magisterial authority. More broadly, the undivided Word of God regenerates believers such that they are able to live undivided lives; that is, lives of peace.

From this perspective, Jesus is not a portable deity who travels with Christians as a kind of good-luck charm or cheerful pal to secure their lives. The relationship between Christians and Jesus is not primarily "personal," although there is a personal dimension. This relationship is not simply a matter of affirming a belief found in the Bible or even accepting the authority of the Bible, although certainly beliefs are involved and the Bible's authority is at stake. Moreover, the presence of Jesus does not make an individual "perfect," as in the Wesleyan holiness doctrine of sanctification, although the regenerative power of the Word of God—the work of Jesus Christ—does open up a path of holiness.

In other words, following Menno's Christology, Jesus is not first of all a possession of the believer; instead, the believer has now become a possession of Jesus Christ. Jesus is the one to whom we have become attached and through whom we have been regenerated insofar as we have been baptized into newness of life in the church. Our membership in Christ's body renews us and restores us because the same incorruptible seed from which Christ was born is the seed from which we have been reborn. Our "perfection" lies in our attachment to Jesus Christ, not in any deeds we are able to perform

---

68. Menno, *Complete Writings*, 554.
69. Menno, *Complete Writings*, 920–21.

as individuals through our corruptible flesh. We are saved in the church, not apart from it. Being without spot or wrinkle is only possible when we are acting as faithful members of Christ's body.

Thus, an important reason why many Christians in North America are living like the world is because they have become primarily of the world, which is to say that they do not spend enough of their life as part of the body of Christ—in the company of Christ's members. To become like Jesus will require that they participate in his life and suffering as members of his body. Such suffering solidarity is not a matter of despising the flesh, as Dennis Martin has accused Menno of teaching, but rather of divining the flesh—making bodies godly.[70]

Menno, in his version of celestial flesh doctrine succeeded in linking the Christ of the atonement with the Christ of the creation, as J. A. Oosterban pointed out back in 1961.[71] Oosterban saw much to praise in Menno's vision of a church wherein believers share Jesus' body, becoming "flesh of his flesh and bone of his bone."[72] And Oosterban also recognized that such a vision had dawned again the writings of the great theologian Karl Barth, who wrote that "the Virgin birth at the opening and the empty tomb at the close of Jesus' life bear witness that this life is a fact marked off from the rest of human life" and that "the mystery at the beginning is the basis of the mystery at the end."[73] Thus, for Barth, as for Menno, the "Holy Spirit by which Jesus was conceived" is the same Spirit by which it "becomes really possible for the creature, for man, to be . . . free for God," and for "flesh, human nature" to be "assumed into unity with the Son of God."[74] And this "freedom which the Holy Spirit gives" is for Barth, as for Menno, "the freedom of the Church, of the children of God."[75] We are saved, in other words, not so much through a personal relationship with Jesus or by acceptance of Jesus Christ as our personal savior, but rather in the church, by the power of the Holy Spirit, and through the birth, death, and resurrection of Jesus Christ—the Word who became flesh and dwelt among us.

For Menno, this body of Christ—the people of God—is intrinsically nonviolent because its very existence is defined by allegiance to the prince

---

70. Martin, "Menno and Augustine," 43–51.
71. Oosterbaan, "Theology of Menno Simons," 192.
72. Oosterbaan, "Theology of Menno Simons," 195.
73. Barth, *Church Dogmatics*, I.2, 182–83.
74. Barth, *Church Dogmatics*, I.2, 199.
75. Barth, *Church Dogmatics*, I.2, 198.

of peace, rather than to the prince of strife: "We who were formerly no people at all and who knew of no peace are now called to be such a glorious people of God, a church, kingdom, inheritance, body, and possession of peace."[76] As is the prince, so is the kingdom, in Menno's theology: "With this King, and in his Kingdom and reign, it is nothing but peace. Everything that is seen, heard, and done is peace."[77] The nonviolent Word of God, as made visible in the life, death, and resurrection of Jesus Christ, is now visible also in the people who have been regenerated from this incorruptible seed—a people of God's peace, a new creation.[78]

---

76. Menno, *Complete Writings*, 555.

77. Menno, *Complete Writings*, 554.

78. See "We Are People of God's Peace," a hymn based on the passages quoted in this paragraph. *Hymnal: A Worship Book*, #407.

── Part Two ──

Anabaptists and the Contemporary Believers Church

Introduction

Defining Anabaptism

ANABAPTISTS IN THE TIME of the Reformation had ideas that were considered revolutionary and dangerous.[1] When they read words attributed to Jesus in Matt 28:19 about making disciples and then baptizing, they decided that the placement of "making disciples" before baptism meant that people had to be taught about being a disciple of Jesus, and that meant becoming a disciple required making a decision. The conclusion followed that those making that decision would be adults.[2] As a result these nascent Anabaptists rejected baptism of infants and moved to institute baptism of adults. Soon what originated as a reform of baptism led to the beginning of what in the sixteenth century seemed like a new form of church, namely a church modeled on the example of Jesus as recounted in Scripture as the primary source of theology and ethics. It was a church composed of faithful believers who chose to join as adults, which made it independent of both the civil government and the church of the masses that government authorities had established. Since it was commonly assumed that the faith of

---

1. For a book-length, popular version of the origin of sixteenth-century Anabaptism, see Weaver, *Becoming Anabaptist* and also Mast and Weaver, *Defenseless Christianity*, 15–71.

2. For important discussion of Erasmus as the sixteenth-century origin of this interpretation and its route to Anabaptists, see Friesen, *Erasmus, the Anabaptists*.

the church established by civil authority undergirded the fabric of society, authorities both civil and ecclesial saw Anabaptists as a threat to the social order. They were considered dangerous, and people who held these beliefs were sometimes, even frequently, executed. We remember them today as Anabaptist martyrs for the faith. Many of their stories appear in *Martyrs Mirror*.[3] Some of these stories appeared in part 1.

Baptizing adults and a church composed of those who chose to belong seemed like new ideas in the sixteenth century. This newly appearing form of church was actually a continuation of the church of Pentecost and of all gatherings of believers since then where Jesus is made visible. However, it seemed new in the context of the sixteenth century, and for ease of reference we have described it as new in the following discussion.

Living in a new church based on the example of Jesus provoked other questions about the medieval churchly tradition that Anabaptists had inherited. Anabaptists read Jesus' words about bread and wine at the last supper as exemplary or symbolic and rejected the sacramental idea that the bread and wine turned into the actual body and blood of Jesus. Many, but certainly not all, sixteenth-century participants in this new understanding of church also followed the example of Jesus in rejecting the sword. Eventually, in the debates about use of the sword, those who rejected the sword emerged as the majority, and Anabaptism became known as a pacifist movement.

Anabaptism as Believers Church

In recent decades, additional terminology has developed to describe the church composed of believers who chose to belong as adults, a choice marked by baptism of adults. It has been designated as a "believers church." This terminology fits churches who practice baptism of adults, but whose roots are not in historic or sixteenth-century Anabaptism.

The opposite of a believers church was not an unbelievers church, but one in which infants were baptized and the faith journey began at that juncture. When baptism of adults first emerged In the Reformation as a controversial but defining issue, the establishment of the church for the masses by civil authority meant that baptism of all infants was a civic requirement. Consequently, the difference between the Anabaptist (believers church) and the established church concerned not only the time at which

3. Van Braght, *Bloody Theater; or, Martyrs Mirror*.

water baptism was administered, but also the matter of choice to belong versus automatic inclusion at birth. In the context of the Reformation, the difference was obvious between Anabaptists (as a believers church) and the established state church.

Besides instituting a new form of church, the matter of choosing baptism as an adult had far-reaching religiopolitical consequences. Baptism as an adult choice undermined the church-state alliance and the assumption that the church supported and assisted the state's use of the sword. A church based in Jesus and separate from state and government had greater potential to follow Jesus in rejecting the sword.

The situation has changed markedly today. In Canada and the United States, there is no church of the masses or state or established church. In a sense, every church is a believers church since each person who attends church does so on the basis of an individual choice. Those baptized as infants who maintain a church identity as adults do so, not because it is a civil requirement, but rather as a voluntary, adult decision to be part of a community of faith. Some might claim that this state of affairs means that the Anabaptists have won, and that it makes little sense today to talk about a believers church. However, other issues raised by the believers church idea are still relevant. The Anabaptists as a believers church whose highest loyalty is to Jesus posed a challenge to the social order. And the church modeled on Jesus today is still called to challenge or pose a witness to the social order. We believe that our current context calls for us to continue to claim the Anabaptist legacy of the church based on Jesus that challenges the social order and thus strives to witness to the presence of the reign of God in a world that does not yet acknowledge the rule of God.

Since the term "Anabaptist" has connotations of a particular historical movement, the term "believers church" remains useful, particularly for traditions with different or even established church roots that nonetheless display Anabaptist characteristics. Examples might be the Christian base communities within Roman Catholicism; or the Episcopalians who told me (Denny) that they recognize that they should put more distance between themselves and the government than has been the case in the past. For additional reasons discussed in a following chapter, the designation believers church applies to African American churches.

PART TWO: ANABAPTISTS AND THE CONTEMPORARY BELIEVERS CHURCH

A Contemporary Update

It is also the case, to state the obvious, that the challenges to the social order today differ significantly from those faced by early Anabaptists. In the United States the challenge will confront society's pervasive faith in violence to solve problems; the claim to "American exceptionalism" as a unique nation blessed by God; the claim that the United States is a "Christian nation" that can force certain "Christian" beliefs on all citizens, such as opposition to abortion, suppression of people who are lesbian, gay, bisexual, transgender or queer (LGBTQ), and support for teaching of young earth and six-day creation as science alongside evolution. Other areas of challenge might include tax policies that favor the rich at the expense of the poor; the continued sexual objectification of women and limitations on their roles in society; a criminal justice system that appears to focus destructively on people of color; hostility to immigrants; racism and assumptions of white superiority (which are discussed in a following chapter), and more.[4] These challenges are relatively visible, and reflect the church's interaction with the social order.

Along with these contemporary challenges, in the nearly five centuries since the Reformation there have been new learnings and advances in the social sciences, in our understandings for the study of history and theology, and in our understandings of the Bible and the methodology used in biblical interpretation. Even as we stand in the Anabaptist tradition, such developments mean that we cannot simply import and reproduce the early Anabaptist movement in our time. In addition, implications of the church that lives in the story of Jesus not apparent in the sixteenth century are manifesting themselves today.

The chapters in part 2 reflect recent understandings. They constitute an updating of Anabaptism and the development of some of these implications. The first chapter in part 2 deals with understandings of Scripture and biblical interpretation, and their implications for discussion of theology and ethics. In part 1, the Anabaptist understanding of the Word was described as a dynamic force active in the world. In the first chapter of part 2, we suggest that a contemporary equivalent to the Word of God made visible in our twenty-first-century context is the "grain of the universe." This concept comes from the belief that God is revealed in the life, teaching, death and resurrection of Jesus, and that the character of God will then be visible

---

4. These and other issues are discussed in Weaver, *God Without Violence*, and in Weaver, *Education with the Grain*.

in the grain of the universe God created, for those who look at the world through eyes focused by the story of Jesus. The grain of the universe carries over and becomes visible in following chapters, which develop some additional implications not specifically recognized for Anabaptism in the sixteenth century. One chapter describes black churches as believers churches and then sketches what white churches can learn from black theology, and the importance of dialogue between historically black and white believers churches. The final chapter deals with nonviolent activism as an extension of the church's witness to the world and is thus integral to the discussion of how the church confronts injustice in its host society.

CHAPTER 4

The Nonviolent Grain of the Bible

The Word and the Story

Introduction

SIXTEENTH-CENTURY ANABAPTISTS SET IN motion a movement whose implications we are still discovering. They appealed to the story of Jesus and to the Scriptures that contained that story. By appealing to the story of Jesus, Anabaptist readers were also giving authority to the life of Jesus Christ, a life that is most vividly and fully displayed in a narrative, more than in an abstract set of principles or truth statements. By giving voice and shape to the life and teachings of Jesus, the story of Jesus functioned as the Word of God, a dynamic force in the world that confronts violence and injustice and offers new possibilities for reconciliation and restoration. Previous chapters in part 1 displayed some examples of how Anabaptists read the Bible in this way—as the revelation of a nonviolent and dynamic Word on the move.

However, contemporary scholars—Anabaptist and otherwise—do not interpret the Bible as did early Anabaptists, since we live in a different context and bring new discoveries from several centuries of biblical studies to the task of interpretation. In other words, twenty-first-century Anabaptists—and Christians more generally—have a different hermeneutics than those who were reading and discussing the Bible in the sixteenth century. This difference provokes several questions. Since we live in different times and use different methodology, what does it mean to stand in the line of sixteenth-century Anabaptism, or to claim the name of these particular Reformation leaders? Put differently, once the direction of biblical understanding found in sixteenth-century Anabaptism is identified, how can we keep it moving in the same direction even though our cultural setting is dramatically different? Put simply, what is a modern version of Anabaptist biblical theology?

The history from an earlier epoch cannot simply be copied; it cannot be transported across centuries and transplanted in the present time. Neither can contemporary theology build extensively on earlier statements as unquestioned givens—that would be to stop historical movement at the time of the earlier epoch. However, studying the past is important because it helps us see "that the way things are is the result of a process, not a natural law," as Rowan Williams has said.[1] In the case of Anabaptism, we study the movement in order to understand the process of thought and action that led to its challenge of the religious and social systems of sixteenth-century Europe. In so doing, we are able to identify the direction in which the new movement was pointing, and to the extent that we identify with that movement, the contemporary task is one of contextually authentic fidelity; that is, to stay committed to the movement in a way that is up to date, or to keep it moving in the same direction in our particular context.

This chapter is thus a sketch of such a contemporary updating of an Anabaptist perspective on the story from Scripture of Jesus who made present in his life and teaching the reign of God. In the language of John 1, this story, together with the life it displays, is called the Word of God. Today this Word can be identified with the grain of the universe—that thread of life in our cosmos that channels the creativity of divine power against violence and death that sometimes seem to rule the universe.

Although this sketch is called an Anabaptist perspective, it is also an ecumenical text. As is explained more extensively below, since the import of the Anabaptist movement was to point back to Jesus, and since all Christians proclaim faith in Jesus as Savior, pointing to the story of Jesus as the basis of faith actually presents an ecumenical perspective, open and addressed to every Christian.

The Narrative of Jesus

In contemporary understanding, appealing to the story of Jesus is a multifaceted process. It seems clear that the earliest appeals to Jesus and the earliest way of identifying Jesus was to tell his story. That was the approach taken by the apostles in the weeks following Jesus' death and resurrection when the apostles were asked in whose name they were speaking and acting. We

---

1. Williams, *Why Study the Past*, 25.

find their answers in the book of Acts, in 2:14–39; 3:13–26; 4:10–12; 5:30–32; 10:36–43; 13:17–41. Each of these texts presents an outline of the life, death, and resurrection of Jesus, often including indications of how his story is linked to the history of Israel. As long as the story was still in the living memory of the apostles' audience, the apostolic speakers needed only to refer to the outline. But when the eye witnesses to Jesus began to die, the Gospels were written to fill in the outline and preserve the story for later generations. In the Gospels we have four versions of the story. These accounts agree for the most part but differ in a number of specific, seemingly contradictory details. To appeal to Jesus, as sixteenth-century Anabaptists did, is to reference this story. The arc of the story, from birth to resurrection, including the variations in detail, is the story to which contemporary Anabaptists appeal, just as did their sixteenth-century counterparts.

The focus on the story of Jesus sets up a complex relationship between Jesus and the text that contains his story. Jesus is the highest source of appeal or the highest authority for Christians. The text that contains that story is obviously authoritative, but the text itself is not Jesus. Thus the story of Jesus and the person of Jesus depicted in the words of Scripture is our ultimate authority. This story is the saving message of the gospel, the Word of God. Stated another way, Jesus the Christ is the Word of God, and the words of Scripture are a witness to that saving Word. As we study and seek to obey the Scriptures together with our brothers and sisters in Christ, the story of Jesus becomes alive to us in such a way that the Bible itself can speak to us, can make the Word of God present to us. In that sense we can experience the Bible as "the Word of God written." However, the words on the page should not be mistaken for the Word made flesh who came to dwell among us (John 1:14). Otherwise we risk a form of idolatry—worshiping a book rather than the One to whom the book bears witness.

As the apostles did, we too should begin our identification of Jesus by telling his story.[2] But even as we use Acts and the four Gospels for our primary data on that story, we must recognize that identifying Jesus is always to some extent an interpretative process—an active and lively reception of the story of Jesus in our own setting with its particular challenges and possibilities.

---

2. For longer sketches of this story, including summaries of Jesus' actions and teaching, see Weaver, *God Without Violence*, ch. 1, and Weaver, *Education with the Grain*, ch. 1.

The Process of Interpretation

Identifying Jesus and learning to know him by telling and hearing his story is an interpretative process. We see that process—at least the beginning of that interpretative process—already in the details that differ among the four Gospels. The Gospels were not written at the same time, and each of the Gospel writers told the story in a way that reflected his particular context and concerns. For example, Matthew emphasized Jesus' location within the story of Israel while Luke emphasized the meaning of Jesus for all nations. Or, when the Gospel writers cited one of Jesus' parables, endings could differ, as in the parable of the Wedding Banquet in Matt 22:1–14 and Luke 14:15–24. The fact that the writers differed, we suggest, shows how they shaped and applied—interpreted—the story for their particular purposes. And with these differences in view, it should be clear that the shape of the story in its details is never final.

There is one specific dimension in the process of interpretation that primarily accounts for the differences among the four Gospels: the context of their proclamation. This same dimension explains differences in biblical interpretation today: the external context within which contemporary people read the Bible changes over time, and differs from one culture to another. Such shifts mean that the questions we bring to the story change, and the way that we understand and apply the story changes. Thus identifying and knowing Jesus by telling his story requires acknowledging that the process is open ended and never finished.

I (Denny) grew up, for example, with the words of Jesus from the King James Bible ringing in my ears: "Resist not evil" (Matt 5:39). In my Mennonite denomination, that particular phrase was interpreted to require "nonresistance," a stance that today appears to be a passive approach toward all evil—to remain quiet and accept without resistance an injustice such as racial segregation. The example from Jesus cited would have been his conduct at his trial. In the Mennonite context of my youth, this approach can be understood as supporting Mennonite withdrawal from society and purity from the corruption of the surrounding world. From this point of view, as a teenager during the Civil Rights Movement, I thought that Martin Luther King Jr. was engaged in resistance and therefore violating the command and example of Jesus. But in college, after coming to understand better the evil of racial segregation, and becoming better informed about King's nonviolent movement, combined with being awakened to the nonviolent activism of Jesus who healed on the Sabbath, cleansed the temple and more, I came to see that the story of Jesus lends clear support to nonviolent activism as a way to make God's reconciling rule visible over against systemic injustice as well as direct violence. A later chapter in this book expands on the idea of Jesus nonviolent activism and its relevance for today. But this idea of nonviolent activism makes sense in a context where we now understand that part of the church's mission is to challenge the injustice of society, not just to withdraw from such injustice, although such withdrawal can be a good first step.

For other examples of contextual changes that make a difference in biblical interpretation, consider how the relationship between Anabaptist churches and pedobaptist churches might look different in the sixteenth-century context of a mass church as distinguished from the contemporary United States and Canada where every church is in a sense a believers church. Or how the church based on Jesus should relate to political authorities in the United States or Canada, where there is freedom of religion and freedom to protest, in contrast to the situation in a totalitarian state such as the old German Democratic Republic; or a state in which Islam is the official religion; or one in which only certain churches are recognized. Such examples could be extended greatly. The point here is that how to understand who Jesus is and what it means to be his disciple is an open-ended discussion. We are always in the process of understanding the meaning of the story—interpreting—and how and what it means to live in his story.

The Old Testament

In several ways, recognizing the story of Jesus as our beginning point and source of authority gives reality and significance to the story of Israel in the Old Testament. That story began with the Patriarch Abraham and it flows through Jesus.

In some of the previously mentioned six sermons in Acts, the apostolic speaker recounted versions of the history of Israel in order to situate Jesus as a continuation of that story. In the account of Jesus walking with the two disciples on the road to Emmaus, Luke 24:27 reports that Jesus interpreted the Scriptures to them about himself from Moses (the Pentateuch) and the prophetic writings. Later in the same chapter it is reported that Jesus opened these same Scriptures during an appearance to the eleven remaining disciples and their companions. These accounts in which both Jesus and the apostles put the story of Jesus in the continuation of the Old

Testament make clear that what Christians call the Old Testament belongs integrally to the Bible for Christians.

The historical writings of the Old Testament bear the same kind of discrepancies in details that we see in the Gospels. Genesis 1 and 2 have different stories of creation. There are two intermingled accounts of the flood story in Genesis. Variations and double recitations occur in stories of the Patriarchs; details differ for the same events between Kings and Chronicles. Clearly the Old Testament, as well as the Bible as a whole, is not a seamless, integrated document. It contains a variety of kinds of literature, and it reflects the fact that its contents were written over a period of many centuries by many authors who reflect a variety of contexts and understandings. Centuries later these writings were assembled into one collection that we call the Bible. Given the circumstances of its creation, it is not at all surprising that the biblical writings contain paradoxes and contradictions, and that our interpretative efforts are always to some extent open ended and on going.

Divine Violence and Nonviolence

One of the most important of contradictions in the Old Testament—we will call it a conversation—concerns violence and the role of God in that violence. Well known are the many wars and massacres said to be commanded by the God of Israel. Among the most familiar such stories are the conquest of Jericho and the massacres that accompanied the conquest of Palestine as reported in Joshua 1–11, and the wars of David (2 Sam 8).

Equally as well known as the references to violence but not often linked together to form a pattern are stories of actors who used creative ways to avoid violence, often with divine assistance, or stories that reflect a God who avoids violence. These texts include the nonviolent creation accounts of Genesis 1 and 2, a nonviolence that jumps into view when the biblical accounts are compared with the chaos and violence perpetrated by the gods in the Babylonian account of the creation of heavens and earth in the epic *Enuma Elish*; Isaac's refusal to fight over wells (Gen 26); the noncompliance by the Hebrew midwives with the directives to kill all male babies (Exod 1); Gideon's use of a ruse to rout the Midianites (Judg 7); Abigail's intervention to prevent a war (1 Sam 25); Elisha's repelling of an Aramean invasion with a feast (2 Kgs 6); nonviolent cultural resistance by Hebrew captives (Daniel); and the displaying of God's mercy in Jonah. Dealing with this conversation that contains contrasting views of God and divine assistance adds another dimension to the importance of Jesus for the Old Testament.

Old Testament writers obviously differed among themselves and sometimes even within themselves in how they understood God and God's working in the world. This difference becomes acute in light of the belief that the character of God and the reign of God are revealed in the story of Jesus, which vividly and unequivocally displays a rejection of lethal violence for any purpose, including the divine action on behalf of salvation. In the midst of a conversation about the God of Israel depicted in the Old Testament, one cannot determine the character of God simply by putting a finger on one story or another and repeating it in a loud voice. For Christians at least, recalling that the story of Jesus is a continuation of the story of Israel, however, does shed great light on this conversation. The story and life of Jesus enter a conversation about the God of Israel reflected in the Hebrew Bible, highlighting the nonviolent characteristics of the God of the Bible. Jesus constitutes one side of an unresolved biblical conversation, in other words, a side that in Christian faith and understanding becomes definitive, since Christians follow Jesus Christ as a complete and reliable revelation of the will and character of God.[3] In other words, it was the actors and the writers who depicted alternatives to divine violence that best reflected the God of Israel made present in Jesus Christ.

That is not to say that the violent images of God in the Bible should be rejected or ignored in our interpretation of the Word of God as found in Scripture. These violent images reflect a dimension of how God seems to have acted to those scribes who gave us the Bible; they pose an understanding of God that conflicts with—even as it is in conversation with—the revelation of God in Jesus Christ. When Jesus said, "You have heard it said 'you shall love your neighbor and hate your enemy,' but I say to you 'love your enemies,'" he is making clear the understanding of God he is advocating, as well as the understanding of God he is repudiating. Both of these understandings are available in Scripture, including in the Old Testament, yet the story of Jesus shows us clearly which side of the argument is vindicated by Jesus' life, death, and resurrection. While Jewish scholars might well interpret these Old Testament writings differently; many Jewish scholars recognize that the

---

3. For a full discussion of the conversation in the Old Testament and its resolution in the narrative of Jesus, see Weaver, *Nonviolent God*, chs. 4 and 5; Weaver, *God Without Violence*, chs. 10–13; Weaver, *Education with the Grain*, 125–40. For additional examples of approaches to the Bible that discover a God who rejects violence, see Nelson-Pallmeyer, *Jesus Against Christianity*; Crossan, *God and Empire*; Seibert, *Disturbing Divine Behavior*.

arguments advanced by Jesus are in fact Jewish arguments and they urge Christian interpreters to recognize the deeply Jewish character of Jesus' perspective as well.[4]

An Early Anabaptist Precedent

Dealing with contradictions resolved by the narrative of Jesus has some precedents in sixteenth-century Anabaptists' writings. They were quite aware that the Bible was not a seamless document. They read it carefully and compiled lists of contradictory texts. Understanding the Bible meant coming to terms with such texts. Balthasar Hubmaier supplied two pages of contradictory texts in his tract on justifying use of the sword in spite of the biblical injunction, "You should not kill." Hans Denck listed forty pairs of seemingly contradictory texts, both of which are true. When possessing the truth, he writes, one can reconcile these texts as "one included in the other, as the lesser in the greater, as time in eternity, place in the infinite [*aine wirdt in der andern verschlossen, also das minder im merern, als zeyt in der ewigkait, stat in der unentlichait*]." Ultimately, Denck concluded, we recognize how little we know, and find satisfaction in the "Christ of God our Father [*Christus Gots, unsers vatters*]."[5] Pilgram Marpeck and Leupold Scharnschlager compiled lists of terms that contrast Old and New Testaments, and death and life, the two sides of faith. These lists culminate with references to Wisdom of Solomon 2, and John 3 and 1 Corinthians 15.[6] In the commentary on the Frankenthal Disputation, in a section entitled "Whether the Writings of the Old Testament Are as Valid for Christians as Those of the New," Anabaptists disputed the equation of Old and New Testaments by Reformed theologians, who sought to minimize or render optional Jesus's rejection of the sword. The commentary lists a long series of texts which project differences between Old and New Testaments. In a quite modern sounding resolution of these contrasts, the writers state: "Therefore our greatest certainty is to remain with the words of the Lord Jesus and his holy apostles, through which we have before our eyes a crystal-clear

---

4. See, for example, the work of Levine, *Short Stories by Jesus*.
5. Hubmaier, *Balthasar Hubmaier*, 512–14; Denck, *Schriften*, 2:68–73.
6. This anonymous document was attributed to Michael Sattler and appears in Yoder, *Legacy of Michael Sattler*, 171–73. More recently Marpeck and Scharnschlager were identified as the likely authors. See Packull, "Pilgram Marpeck," 351–55.

differentiation between the Old and New Testament as has already been shown adequately and at length with Holy Scripture."[7]

Our contemporary methods of interpretation do not follow sixteenth-century hermeneutics. The approach we have sketched certainly differs from these early Anabaptists. However, these early Anabaptists provide a precedent for recognizing that the biblical text contains contradictions, and that some of them eventually found a resolution in Jesus Christ. In these Anabaptist writings there is also a precedent for seeing the Old Testament as part of Christian Scriptures linked to the New Testament. And by pointing to the conversation about understanding divine violence and the character of God, with a resolution in the narrative of Jesus, we can carry forward the biblical legacy of early Anabaptists in our time and place.

Additional Old Testament Issues

The argument that the narrative of Jesus points to one side of the conversation in the Old Testament about the character of God is more than merely a modern interpretation. It bears resemblance to the previously noted way that New Testament writers connected the story of Jesus to the early sacred Scriptures (our Old Testament), a connection visible in statements by the apostles in the book of Acts, as well as in the accounts of Jesus' use of the Old Testament, and then in later New Testament writers,

As noted before, identifying some parts of the Old Testament as portraying a view of God not sanctioned by the narrative of Jesus is in no way a rejection of parts of it. On the contrary. The violent texts are necessary; without them we would not see the conversation. Seeing that the conversation exists and that Jesus resolves the contradiction adds to the significance of the story of Jesus. If the violent elements of the story in the Old Testament were suppressed, that element of the significance of Jesus would be missing.

This approach stands in contrast to another effort to argue that the God of Israel in the Old Testament is a nonviolent God. This alternative affirms that the nonviolent character of God is revealed in Jesus, but then argues that even the texts with divine violence should be interpreted in such a way that they also point to a nonviolent God. We instead argue that allowing the violent texts to stand as testament to a belief in a God who resorts to violence actually takes the violence depicted in the text of the Old

---

7. Snyder, *Later Writings of the Swiss Anabaptists*, 255–70, quote 267–68.

Testament more seriously than interpreting the violent texts so that they point away from a violent God.

Further, we already observed that the Word of God is ultimately Jesus Christ, and that the text of the Gospels is a witness to that Word. We can now extend those observations to the Old Testament as well. The text itself is not the Word; rather the text witnesses to God and God's Word that appears in Jesus. It is Jesus who helps us to discover that the Word present in Jesus is also present in the Old Testament.

Some of the texts that proclaim violent, divine judgment or celebrate seeming divine vengeance on enemies, particularly texts in the prophetic literature or Psalms, can be interpreted to affirm from a reverse angle the rejection of violence by the God made visible in Jesus. Violence is cyclical, violence begets violence, or as the saying goes, "What goes around comes around." These texts suggest that violence and corruption breeds more violence and corruption—a fitting punishment for perpetrators. See for example in Psalm 7, where God is said to be whetting his sword of judgment on the wicked, but then this judgment is described as follows: "They make a pit, digging it out, and fall into the hole that they have made. Their mischief returns upon their own heads, and on their own heads their violence descends" (vv. 15–16). In Psalm 9, this understanding of God's judgment is confirmed: "The nations have sunk in the pit that they made; in the net that they hid has their own foot been caught. The Lord has made himself known, he has executed judgment; the wicked are snared in the work of their own hands" (vv. 15–16). Following the theological vision of Psalm 7 and 9, we suggest that texts that celebrate God's vengeance or that declare destruction as divine punishment can be interpreted as statements of the way violence breeds violence, and as declarations of what happens when God's way is rejected. They are statements of what occurs when people or societies continue on their own violent or destructive paths. This claim is the other side of saying that the way of the God revealed in Jesus is to reject violence.

At the same time, we should recall that the Bible contains a variety of kinds of literature, composed over a very long period of time. It is unrealistic to think that we can integrate every last text into one seamless piece. Nonetheless, a long-running saga does provide the unity of the Bible. This is the story of Israel, the story that enters world history with Abraham, continues in the history of Israel, and passes through and reaches a new stage with the story of Jesus as Messiah, and then continues on into the early church. With this story in mind, we can find evidence of the God revealed in Jesus all along the story of Israel that unfolds throughout the Bible.

The disparate accounts in the Bible, particularly in the Old Testament, do allow people from diverse perspectives to draw support from a variety of texts. For example, James Cone, a founder of the Black Theology Movement, appeals to the story of the Exodus to understand God as a liberator, providing a framework for understanding the work and mission of Jesus as a revelation of this God who is a liberator. In contrast, prominent womanist theologian Delores Williams highlights the story of Hagar, the slave of Abraham's wife Sarah. For a time Hagar was expelled from Abraham's household and then eventually told by an "angel of the Lord" to return to Abraham's tents. Williams uses this story to argue that God is not always liberator; at times, God provides support in the midst of suffering.[8]

As the discussion in this section displays, the early Anabaptist impulse of appealing to the story of Jesus as norm or beginning point can find significant parallels in our contemporary understanding of the Bible. The following section extends that discussion into the realm of theology that is derived from the narrative of Jesus.

Theology

The idea of "beginning with Jesus," namely that our ultimate commitment is to the Jesus of the gospel story, has profound implications for understanding the character of theology. Theology is the language that we use to extract meaning from or to extend the significance of the story. The first instances of the process of extracting meaning from the story appear already with the sermons in Acts. When the apostles told the story and then added that resurrection established Jesus as Lord and Messiah, or that this story blotted out sins, or was the source of salvation, or that belief in it brought forgiveness of sins, they were doing theology. That is, they were drawing meaning out of the story that is not stated explicitly in the events of the story.

The first theological writings of any length about Jesus that we know of are the New Testament epistles by the Apostle Paul.[9] When we draw

---

8. See Cone, *God of the Oppressed*, and Williams, *Sisters in the Wilderness*.

9. It is worth nothing that Paul did not see himself as a Christian starting a new religion. He was rather a devout Jew who believed that Jesus was the Messiah, the Christ. It was later that this belief was claimed as Christian.

meaning from or extend the significance of the story of Jesus, we are following in the footsteps of the apostles and of Paul and doing what they did. That is not to equate our words with the words of Scripture. What gives their words specific significance is their proximity to the story of Jesus and to those who knew Jesus personally. Nonetheless, in our theological efforts we are engaged in the same practice that Paul (and other New Testament writers) performed, namely drawing meaning from and extending the story of Jesus.

Several points follow from this observation. For one, the process of drawing meaning from the narrative of Jesus is always open ended, as stated before. Since contexts change over time or from one culture to another, it is evident that new questions arise and thus the process of explaining who Jesus is and what he means in the new context is always open ended. We are always in the process of understanding Jesus' story and what it means in our context.

The fact that the meaning of the story—our theology—is always under discussion, means that theology is never finished. Stated differently, since theology is an expression of the meaning of Jesus in a particular context, starting with the story of Jesus relativizes all theology. In other words, theology is always relative to a particular context; it reflects the context in which it is articulated, and it is not possible to develop a theology that will transcend human particularity and apply to all people in all times and places both in the past and the future.

The claim that no theological formulas or statements escape particularity includes the classic creeds and formulas, in particular the statements from the Councils of Nicea, Constantinople, and Chalcedon, and the trinitarian formula suggested by the three Cappadocian Fathers. Although it is common to ignore the worldviews and philosophical system in which these formulas were at home, and to treat them as unquestioned, transcendent givens, these formulas were in fact produced by men and emerged from a particular context that they reflect. Historians trace the first appearance of the ideas and the paths taken until they reached their final status. In that particular context, they were true statements, working within the world view and philosophical assumptions of that age. However, since we live in a very different world view and context, we can learn from these creeds and formulas but are not beholden to them for our own understanding of and formulations about Jesus. In other words, an understanding of Christology should begin with a discussion of the character and identity of Jesus in his story rather than with efforts to make Nicea and Chalcedon and Cappadocian trinitarian terminology relevant for today.

Examples of rethinking theology with respect to the narrative of Jesus appear already in writings of sixteenth-century Anabaptists. Chapters in part 1 of this book display a number of examples in which these writers began to consider new ways of talking about Jesus that reflected their understanding of a church based on the model of Jesus. The appendix on trinitarianism's usage in *Martyrs Mirror* cites other examples of theological expression not wholly dependent on classic statements.

On occasion, early Anabaptists did quote the classic creedal statements and formulas. Some writers have cited this usage as evidence that Anabaptists were not original thinkers and merely repeated the inherited theology. That assertion is not altogether true. Anabaptists did not typically cite these classic statements as uniquely authoritative beyond revision. They often added to the statements or interpreted and qualified them in ways that reflected Anabaptist convictions. On occasions, such as in Peter Riedeman's commentary on the creed in his confession of 1565, the original statement virtually disappeared under these additions.[10]

Stated one more way, what Christians have in common is Jesus Christ. Unity should be discovered not in agreeing to certain formulations about Jesus written some centuries after Jesus—even time-honored creeds—but in living out the story of Jesus as disclosed by the Gospels in the life of the church today. This Jesus is a person who is followed. This is the Jesus of the Sermon on the Mount; the Jesus who challenged abuses of the Sabbath, who raised the status of Samaritans and women, and protested the sacrificial system of the temple rulers; the Jesus who told Peter to put away his sword, and who told Pilate that his (Jesus') kingdom was "not from here." Gathering around this Jesus is where the unity of the church should be found today. This is a unity that crosses denominational lines, and can even make common cause in strategic alliances around specific projects with those who adhere to other faiths.

The Grain of the Universe

For Christians, the narrative of Jesus, which we have in multiple versions in the New Testament, is the most thorough revelation of the reign of God

---

10. Examples of this approach to the classic creeds are found throughout Biesecker-Mast, *Separation and the Sword*.

on earth in the time of Jesus. That story can be called the Word of God, even though it can more precisely be understood as the definitive revelation of the Word of God that continues to be operative in the world—a thread of life and ray of light amid the death and darkness of the cosmos. As the revelation of the reign of God, that story of Jesus found in the Gospels reveals how the world works, and is thus the basis for applying the story to our twenty-first-century world.

A contemporary phrase, "the grain of the universe," expresses the meaning of the story in our world. The grain of the universe—the way the world works when responsive to its own source and life—is revealed in the story of Jesus, whose arc goes from birth through his life and teachings to death and resurrection. The chapters of part 1 sketched sixteenth-century Anabaptist understandings of Word. Grain of the universe functions as a contemporary updating of the Word for the twenty-first century.

John Howard Yoder wrote that "people who bear crosses," that is, identify with the life of Jesus, "are working with the grain of the universe."[11] If God is truly revealed in the New Testament's narrative of Jesus, as we believe it is, then that story reveals the grain of the universe God created, that is, how the universe truly works as an ecology of life and light. In the New Testament version of this grain, it became visible when Jesus confronted injustices related to Sabbath observance and treatment of the poor and sick, when he confronted prejudice against Samaritans and raised the status of women. The grain became visible when Jesus pronounced forgiveness of sins and taught and practiced reconciliation, and most certainly when he refused to take the sword to instigate a violent rebellion against the hated Roman occupiers. This grain was clearly visible at his trial when he told Pilate, "My kingdom is not of this world, . . . not from here" (John 18:36), that is, it has different values than Pilate's kingdom.

Since the reign of God is revealed in the story of Jesus, when we observed that the nonviolent accounts in the Old Testament continue in Jesus, we discover that nonviolent reconciling image of God in the writings of the Old Testament as well, which means that the entire Bible reveals the grain of the universe when we have eyes to see, when we read with eyes focused by the narrative of Jesus. And the faithful church, which attempts to live in and live

---

11. Yoder, "Armaments and Eschatology," 58. A similar idea is Martin Luther King Jr.'s statement, "The arc of the moral universe is long, but it bends toward justice." King, "Where Do We Go from Here?," 199. With the use of Yoder's language, it is also important to recognize the many women who suffered abuse from Yoder.

out of the story of Jesus today, continues to witness to and to make visible the grain of the universe as the Word of God in our contemporary world.

Some precedents exist in early Anabaptism for seeing the character of God in the natural order, akin to the idea that those who bear crosses are working with the grain of the universe. In his tract "On the Mystery of Baptism," Hans Hut wrote about the "gospel of all creatures," which is about "Christ the crucified one." In looking at nature, Hut said, one could see that creatures need to suffer in order to attain their intended end—trees had to be cut in order to become houses, and animals suffer the knife in order to become food. This suffering became an analogy for the "suffering and tribulation which is the work of God" both within and without humans and leads them to salvation.[12] In justifying community of goods in his *Rechenschaft* or *Confession*, Peter Riedemann wrote that "the Creation still testifies today that at the beginning God ordained that people should have nothing individually but should have all things in common with each other." Thus elements of creation that cannot be possessed or controlled or owned by individuals, such as "the sun, the whole course of the heavens, day, air, and so forth" demonstrate God's intent that nothing in creation should belong to individuals.[13] After a lengthy list of biblical texts that he interpreted to support community of goods, Peter Walpot also pointed to "air, rain, snow or water, the sun or other elements" as evidence that God intended for all created things to be held in common.[14] These comments depict Anabaptists making observations about the character of God on the basis of what they see in their surrounding world.

Of course the function of the Word, the grain of the universe, is wider than the explicitly Christian witness. When we have eyes to see, it can be sensed or worked with or its impact discovered in a variety of ways and places. One such example is the fact, verifiable in the social sciences, that violence is cyclical. Using violence does not fundamentally solve a problem; it only extends or postpones it. For example, a riot provokes more police presence, which may produce a forced but momentary calm, but the underlying problem will fester until another incident provokes another riot. A killing to exact vengeance provokes another killing in response. Terrorist attacks do not produce the intended result; instead the country attacked increases its military attacks on suspected agents and the cycle is perpetuated.

---

12. Hut, "On the Mystery of Baptism," 67–72, quotes 67, 69.
13. Riedemann, *Peter Riedemann's Hutterite Confession*, 119, 120.
14. Walpot, "True Yieldedness," 191.

An arms build-up on one side of a conflict provokes a similar response on the other side. And so on. These observations from the so-called real world are evidence that Jesus' words, "Love your enemies, do good to those who hate you" (Luke 6:27), are not merely an ideal that cannot be applied in the so-called real world. On the contrary. Jesus' statement deals with how the world actually works. It is a statement that moving toward peace and reconciliation begins by taking steps to break a cycle of violence and vengeance. Jesus expressed those first steps as showing love for the enemy.

The presence of the grain of the universe is subtle. It becomes visible to eyes focused by the story of Jesus. But since the universe is wider than Christian witness, it is possible for those outside the Christian tradition to sense it, and make it visible with steps taken to halt a cycle of violence. A striking example is Muslim Badshah Khan, who came from a long history of vengeance killings by his Pashtun people in what is today Pakistan in the border region with Afghanistan. Khan came to recognize the futility of the cycle of vengeance killings, and swore himself to nonviolence. He lived with Gandhi and raised a nonviolent force of 100,000 Muslims who marched with Gandhi in the struggle for independence in India.[15]

Other examples illustrate how the grain of the universe becomes visible for those who are willing to see. Quite apart from theological considerations, research evidence in psychology shows that those who forgive are more healthy than those who hang onto anger and pursue vengeance. Research evidence in the social sciences shows that recidivism by offenders is less and perpetrators are rehabilitated more and victims cared for more through processes of restorative justice than when perpetrators are merely punished in conventional retributive justice. These examples illustrate the grain of the universe beyond an explicitly Christian witness, becoming visible as the grain of the universe when we know the story of Jesus and view the world through it. The nonviolence of Jesus that is visible in his life and teaching reflects the grain of the universe—a grain visible when eyes focused by the narrative of Jesus look for it. Stated another way, it takes faith to perceive the grain of the universe.

Jesus' life reveals how the world works, and the grain of the universe is an expression that makes that reality visible in the twenty-first century. This point could be expanded greatly.[16] Following chapters explore two

---

15. Easwaran, *Nonviolent Soldier of Islam*; Pal, *"Islam" Means Peace*, 97–123.

16. For discussion of a series of issues developed from the narrative of Jesus, including discussions of forgiveness and restorative justice, see Weaver, *Education with the*

such applications, in dealing with black and womanist theology, and in advocating nonviolent activism.

Meanwhile, the contemporary idea of the grain of the universe stands in a biblical sequence. Or it can be said to be one more stage in a progression of biblical terms. In Genesis 1, creation happens when God speaks, that is, creation happens with a Word. That spoken, creative Word is then given voice by Wisdom, as in the well-known text of Proverbs 8. Wisdom was with God in the beginning, the first of God's creation, before the beginning of the earth (vv. 22–23). Then follows a sequence of creative events, reminiscent of Genesis 1, in which Wisdom participates (vv. 24–31). In addition, Wisdom is said to speak truth, to gain knowledge, to act prudently, to be the basis of other virtues as well as the source of just rule by kings and nobles (vv. 1–16). Finally, John 1 repeats this sequence of events in which Wisdom participated but now attributes them to the Word, which was in the beginning with God, and everything came into being—was created—through the Word. Then John 1 adds one additional element—"the Word became flesh and lived among us."[17] This Word become flesh was Jesus, the Messiah, the visible manifestation of the reign of God in our world. In his translation of the New Testament, David Bentley Hart brings forward the Greek words "logos"—typically translated "Word"—and "kosmos"—typically translated "world." His translation of John 1:10, which characterizes the mission of the logos or the enfleshed Word, is as follows: "He was in the cosmos, and through him the cosmos came to be, and the cosmos did not recognize him."[18] This translation highlights what we have been trying to say about the cosmic reality of Jesus Christ. The way of Jesus is the Word of God that is the condition of possibility for life and existence, a way and a Word that shines forth amid an uncomprehending darkness and a blind violence.

Consider that everything said about the Wisdom and the Word is also true for the expression, "the Grain of the Universe." This grain is reflected in the universe that God created, and the way the world works when it is alive is revealed in the life, death, and resurrection of Jesus, which is made visible by those who bear crosses, that is, live in the life of Jesus. In the Hebrew and Greek worlds of the Bible, the ideas of wisdom and Word identified what

---

Grain, as well as Weaver, *God Without Violence*. Also illustrating the role of nonviolence in a variety of academic disciplines is Weaver and Biesecker-Mast, *Teaching Peace*.

17. For a detailed account of the link from Genesis 1 to Proverbs 8 to John 1, see Boyarin, *Border Lines*, 96–98.

18. Hart, *New Testament*, 169.

was assumed to be the underlying reality by which the world worked or the foundational essence that held the world together. Today the term "grain of the universe" reflects the profound way the world works when viewed through the story of Jesus as told within our interpretative framework. As sketched very briefly above, the wisdom of rejecting violence as revealed in the story of Jesus is visible in the grain of the universe. The grain of the universe is an ultimate reflection of virtue, and the wisdom by which wise and life-affirming governmental policy decisions are made. In other words, we can see this grain made visible in practices of the faithful church and in every aspect of the cosmos as we study it with eyes of faith. In this book we suggest that the phrase "grain of the universe" is a fitting, contemporary way to express the meaning of Jesus Christ as the Word of God.

Ecumenical Relations

The fact that theology is always open-ended and under discussion has important implications for the relationships among Christians of various contemporary denominations. Since understandings are always under discussion or contingent, there should be no thought of coercion. In other words, the story of Jesus in any interpretation cannot be forced on those unwilling to accept it. The story of Jesus and the good news it contains is thus at heart an intrinsically nonviolent understanding of Jesus and his relevance in our world. The story that cannot be forced on a person against his or her will features a Jesus who rejects violence at its core, who in this specific sense does not resist evil. Ecumenical and interfaith discussions carried out in the light of this story, thus have the character of invitation and witness. Since coercion betrays the very character of the Jesus of the story, the primary form of that witness is the way Christians live. They believe in the story strongly enough to live within the story, to inhabit the story, even when it is costly and dangerous. Living in the story gives a living testimony, a nonverbal or nonrational form of truth telling about the story.

This lived witness points to the close relationship between theology—the words we use to explain who Jesus is—and ethics—the way that Christians live. Both theology and ethics are expressions of the meaning of Jesus—one uses words and language, the other provides a lived version of the meaning of the story, giving witness with practices and bodies. When one wants to know who Jesus is, the answer starts with the story of Jesus.

And when one asks how Christians should live, the answers start with that same story. Theology and ethics are two sides of one proverbial coin.

The relativizing of theology, which was described in a previous section, puts all Christians on a level playing field. Since the story of Jesus belongs to all Christians, making Jesus the foundation on which all Christians build is inherently an ecumenical approach. All denominations and all Christians of whatever constituency are invited to share their understanding of Jesus. Then the story from the Gospels, including the variations in their accounts, is a common frame of reference for discussion of who Jesus is and how to live in his story. Putting everyone on an equal footing when talking about Jesus bypasses arguments about whose founder is more famous or more radical or less orthodox, or which historic creed defines truth for all time—because however we arrived here today we are all talking about Jesus.

Conclusion

Anabaptists were the radicals of the sixteenth century. That is, they went the farthest in rejecting the church of the masses or state church. Since their efforts were considered a threat to the fabric of society, they met frequently with harsh efforts at repression. However, the Anabaptists' impulse of appealing to the story of Jesus and following his rejection of the sword has left a legacy that puts Anabaptism in a very different light today, with implications relevant for all Christians.

The impulse of starting with Jesus or making Jesus the norm of truth makes clear that Jesus Christ is the Word of God, which in turn contributes to our understanding of the character of the Bible. It is a witness to this Word and seeing that Jesus belongs to the history of Israel that makes the Old Testament an indispensable part of the Bible for Christians.

The impulse of starting with Jesus reveals how theology can be described as the words that we use to draw meaning from or apply the story of Jesus in new contexts. That process leads to the understanding that the doing of theology is an open-ended process, always accounting again for the meaning of Jesus in the current context. Stated differently, this means that recognizing Jesus' story as the beginning point for theology relativizes all theological construction. All theology reflects the context in which it is produced, and no theology should be presumed to speak for all people in all contexts both past and present.

Finally, the movement considered the most divisive and radical in the sixteenth century appears today to have the seeds of a specific kind of ecumenical impulse—one based in the foundation of Jesus Christ (1 Cor 3:11). All Christians claim Jesus as Savior and Lord, as Word of God. Claiming Jesus as the beginning point rather than a particular creed or founding leader places all Christians on the same plane to discuss who Jesus is and what it means to be Christians together. With a touch of irony we can say that the movement considered the most divisive in the sixteenth century actually contained the seeds of ecumenism for the twenty-first century.

This relativizing of theology and putting everyone today in the same framework (or on a level playing field)—all of us brothers and sisters in Christ—is the true genius of the Anabaptist movement. In the era of the Reformation, starting with Jesus for Anabaptists led to the development of an understanding of the church new for that time, which was considered quite radical. Only recently have we come to see even more radical implications, namely the relativizing of theology, the invitational character of theology, the equation of word of God and grain of the universe, and the ecumenical dimension of this movement.

In this book we have highlighted the contribution of Anabaptism because for us and our churchly tradition, it has seemed an especially direct, inspirational and clarifying witness to Jesus Christ as our most direct source to the reign of God. But we do not claim that Anabaptism is the only or the necessary source to the good news of forgiveness and reconciliation in the reign of God. We affirm the light—the grain of the universe—wherever it shows up—as in black theology, womanist theology, feminist theology, Amish piety, Catholic monasticism and mysticism, the new monasticism, Protestant liberal activism, Pentecostal pacifism, the emergent church, Seventh-Day Adventist pacifists, LGBTQ nonconformity movements, post-evangelical universalists like Rob Bell, the Girardian peace movement, L'Arche communities, independent sacramental movements, watershed discipleship, Christian socialist communities, and more. We need not agree in all things to find commonality in the story of Jesus and in specific applications of the story that reflect our emphases.

The following chapter demonstrates this ecumenical dimension by showing the benefit of dialogue between mostly white believers churches and historic black churches.

CHAPTER 5

Black and White Believers Churches in Conversation

Introduction

TO DATE SELF-PROFESSED ANABAPTIST churches in North America have been predominantly white churches but only in the last few years has that fact been raised to the level of a problem.[1] When we extend the analysis beyond Anabaptist churches to the larger group of churches that practice baptism by confession of faith—sometimes called believers churches— the picture may seem not to change very much. The usual list of historic believers churches such as Brethren, Baptists, Disciples of Christ, and Assemblies of God have most often been confined to predominantly white denominations. However, in our understanding of the characteristics of a believers church, many historically black churches might also be seen as believers churches. This chapter explores similarities and differences between black churches as believers churches and Anabaptist churches as believers churches. There could be considerable mutual benefit from dialogue between the two, with the white churches having the most to learn. In addition, dealing with racism in this discussion brings out justice-seeking dimensions of the grain of the universe.

Such a conversation is complex, as is exemplified by my (Denny) ongoing discussions with an African American pastor. On the one side, my friend has recently been added to the staff of a quite large, evangelical, white congregation. He has a title in multicultural ministry and worship arts, while his congregation continues to worship as an independent African American satellite of the large white congregation. In this context his concern is to

---

1. Existing in a white context without noticing its whiteness is a sign of white privilege, which is discussed in a bit more detail in what follows.

maintain his congregation's historic African American identity rather than being diffused and absorbed or assimilated into the larger host's outlook. On the other hand, my friend and I have been discussing how to enable a constructive conversation between members of our similar-sized but distinct African American and largely white congregations. Rather than seeking a low common denominator, our goal is to discover how we can learn from and be enriched by the distinct identities of our two congregations. Here the challenge may be for white people to recognize the white privilege and status they bring to a seemingly neutral conversation. These exchanges with my friend reveal some of the complexity of black-white dialogue: confronting multiple aspects of white privilege and dominance, and how minorities, whether religious or ethnic, can maintain their distinct identities without falling into separation or withdrawal.

Great variety exists among both black and white churches with believers church characteristics. For purposes of this chapter, we will speak generically of white believers churches, but we are typically thinking more particularly of Anabaptist varieties of believers churches. For black churches, we will speak generically but also more precisely from the context of American religious history and with attention to black and womanist theology.

Believers Church Characteristics

As explained in the introduction to part 2, the term "believers church" designated a church composed of believers who had made a choice to accept faith as adults, a choice marked by adult baptism. The opposite of believers church was not a church of unbelievers, but a church in which persons began the faith journey as infants and were baptized at that juncture. At the time of the sixteenth-century Reformation, when baptism of adults first emerged at the beginning of the modern era, the church was established and protected by civil authorities, and baptism of infants was a civil requirement. Refusal of infant baptism and practice of adult baptism was a civil crime, often punishable by death. In that context, what today we call a believers church was clearly identifiable. It was a church that challenged the social order into which one was initiated by indiscriminate and mandatory pedobaptism.

However, in contemporary United States and Canada where there is no required state church or church of the masses, every church is in a sense a believers church. That is, regardless of the age of persons baptized, each church is composed of people who belong out of individual choice rather than as a civic requirement.

With the demise of an official state church in the United States,[2] our context has changed markedly from that of the Reformation era. But in our new context, there is still the need for a church that challenges the social order, and can still be designated Anabaptist or "believers church." We use the term to designate a church that seeks to live according to the way of Jesus, which gives it an identity distinct from or over against the social order. This understanding of Jesus as normative for life was a characteristic of sixteenth-century Anabaptists.[3] This definition is by no means limited to churches descended from historic Anabaptism, but it does serve to distinguish churches of this stripe from those who would identify the United States as a "Christian nation," and then describe the Christian duty of believers to support this Christian nation.[4] Such an attitude—rejected by genuine believers churches—treats Christianity as a de facto or unofficial state religion.

Commonalities and Differences

For somewhat different historical reasons, Anabaptists and black churches each have a spiritual identity distinct from the social order, even though there are many in both traditions that prefer not to emphasize this distinct identity. In this section we will highlight three areas of potential overlap between Anabaptist and black church identity—historical and sociological

---

2. In colonial New England, the Puritans arrived with the idea of establishing their form of church, later to be identified as Congregationalism. Further south in Virginia, the Carolinas, and Maryland, the Anglican church was favored. At the federal level, all such churches were disestablished with the First Amendment to the United States Constitution. Disestablishment at the state level occurred gradually, with the last vestiges disappearing in Massachusetts in 1831 and 1833. One response to disestablishment was the host of nineteenth-century voluntary societies—revivalism, temperance, Sunday school, Bible and tract societies, YMCA and YWCA, and more—that sought to spread a Protestant ethos and make the United States a Christian nation on a voluntary basis. The legacy of this impulse is still present in our country today. See Smith et al., *American Christianity*, 2:10–19; Ahlstrom, *Religious History*, 379–80; Beecher, "On Disestablishment in Connecticut," 92–83; Beecher, "Plea for the West," 122–30; Beecher, "Tendencies of American Progress," 235–48.

3. For this description of Anabaptism, see Mast and Weaver, *Defenseless Christianity*.

4. It is frequently the case that this distinction between challenging and accommodating the social order is not clear; many hybrids exist, often with unresolved tensions.

parallels; hermeneutics and approaches to the Bible; and theology. It is important to underscore that differences exist within these parallels. Both similarities and differences contribute to potential learnings from conversation between Anabaptists and black churches.

Historical Parallels

One element of commonality is that Anabaptist churches and black churches have each suffered persecution at the hands of representatives of the dominant social order. In the era of the Reformation, Anabaptists were outlawed. Several thousand met cruel deaths from torture, drowning, fire and more. Such harassment continued into the seventeenth century in some cases, and even after physical torture ended, legal restrictions on Anabaptists continued. Stories of these martyrs appear in *Martyrs Mirror*.[5] This history of suffering and persecution reminds contemporary Anabaptists that their churchly tradition constitutes an often costly challenge to the social order of modern Western societies.

Africans and their descendants in the United States have suffered greatly at the hands of the predominantly white European communities that settled in the North America. They were captured in Africa and brought to North America under cruel and profoundly inhumane conditions. Many of these captives did not survive the passage. From the very earliest European settlements in what is now the United States, white Americans brought Africans to this continent and enslaved them, while establishing a legal system and a political order that protected such slavery. Africans were forced to work without wages for their white owners. Laws both written and implicit governed their every action and kept them in an enslaved condition. Enslavement of these people continued for some 250 years. Enslavement itself was ended with the exceedingly bloody Civil War (1861–65), but racism that undergirded the practice of slavery did not end with the conclusion of this war. Although a period of Reconstruction opened up some new political and economic opportunities for African Americans, within a very few years, a backlash of white supremacist violence and virulently racist laws combined to disempower African Americans and to maintain their second class status. This backlash included the formation of the Ku Klux Klan and similar organizations that practiced terrorism, as well as the development of rigid racial segregation systems and rules designed to suppress black

---

5. Van Braght, *Bloody Theater; or, Martyrs Mirror*.

voting. Resistance to such systems and rules could lead to the horrific death of lynching, which served as an accepted, extra legal practice designed to terrorize black people into submission. Nearly four thousand African American men and women were lynched, with the majority between the 1880s and the 1920s, but some were recorded into the 1960s. Even as legal segregation ended with the Civil Rights Movement, practices have remained whose purpose was to remind people of color of their supposed second-class status. For example, the "war on drugs" has focused primarily on people of color although white people offend at the same rate.[6]

It is important to underscore the obvious, namely that these two histories of suffering are not equal. Anabaptists chose a faith commitment that resulted in persecution. Anabaptists chose to be baptized and to reject the mass church with full awareness that their action was illegal and could result in suffering or death. In contrast, nothing about the suffering of African Americans was voluntary. Even after emancipation and the abolition of slavery, the racism that undergirded slavery continued. Still today practices and attitudes remain that remind African Americans that they are different from or stand over against the dominant white culture of United States society.[7]

The contrast between these two experiences of suffering is exacerbated by the fact that the majority of Anabaptists in the United States can justifiably claim minority status, but are also of north European background. They can thus identify with and immerse themselves in the dominant white culture of American society in a way that is difficult for African Americans to accomplish.[8] It is important to acknowledge this two-faceted dimension of Anabaptist experience, which implicates them in the white privilege of their churches as well as of United States culture generally.

With full awareness of the differences as well as the historical parallels of Anabaptist and black churches, the fact that both groups are spiritually

---

6. For an illustrated history of lynching, see Allen, *Without Sanctuary*. A moving theological discussion of lynching in comparison with the crucifixion of Jesus is Cone, *Cross and the Lynching Tree*. For a devastating analysis of the war on drugs, see Alexander, *New Jim Crow*.

7. Significant literature exists that describes this white culture and the white privilege that it fosters. For a short introduction, see McIntosh, "White Privilege," and Fountain, "No Fare." For book-length discussions, helpful are Wise, *Dear White America*; Irving, *Waking up White*; Hart, *Trouble I've Seen*.

8. For a more extensive treatment of this minority and majority status, see Hart, *Trouble I've Seen*, and Hart, "Salvaging Mennonite Theological Education," 74–86.

distinct from the dominant social order of North America has potential for significant mutual learning.

Grain of the Universe Made Visible

If people who bear crosses are working with the grain of the universe, the accounts of Anabaptist and black church suffering contribute to making that grain visible, but in quite different ways. As noted previously, Anabaptists chose a way that led to suffering and persecution. To the extent that they identified with the life of Jesus, that is, bore the cross of Christ, they were working with and giving visibility to the grain of the universe.

Black church suffering has other roots, and their witness to the grain of the universe is of a different but exceedingly significant kind. Africans and African Americans as a whole suffered not because they were Christians but because of their skin color. It was not white. Many died in the passage from Africa to North America, and those who survived that passage endured great degradation in the system of chattel slavery. Yet somehow, many enslaved Africans did survive that ordeal.

Early womanist writers—often channeling slave narratives and spirituals—attributed that survival in the face of monumental evil to the power of God. They articulated that understanding of God via an understanding of theodicy.[9] According to the standard view of theodicy, an omnipotent God controls everything that happens. This assumption reflects the position of those who occupy the dominant status in society; they envision God in their controlling image. In that perspective, God is in charge of evils, such as slavery, as well as the many good things in our world. This view leads to the question, "How can a supposedly good and loving God allow evil and suffering in the world?" Some, particularly those in dominant roles in society, consider the question and decide that evils such as slavery are within the providence of God, and thus should be accepted. Others consider the question and decide that they cannot accept a God who allows an evil such as slavery, and they become atheists. A third answer is that God is weak, and cannot restrain evil.

Womanists described a fourth answer. They observed that enslaved people who had no control over their lives nonetheless believed in God.

---

9. For womanist discussions of theodicy, see Martin, "Biblical Theodicy"; Kirk-Duggan, "African-American Spirituals"; Cannon, "Wounds of Jesus"; Terrell, *Power in the Blood?*, 142–44; Baker-Fletcher, *Dancing with God*, chs. 4–6.

Making use of the slaveholder's Bible, they discovered their own lives in the biblical story of God's liberation of the Hebrews from Egyptian slavery. These enslaved men and women believed that their very existence testified to the power of God, that it was God who enabled them to survive the evil of slavery. In this view, evil originated not with God but with human beings. The evil of slavery was the direct creation of white people, and a good God opposed this evil, opening paths to freedom for slaves and confronting slave-owners with the consequences of their iniquities. Enslaved people were Christians because they believed that the God who liberated the Israelites from Egypt was the God of Jesus the liberator, and it was this God that enabled their survival.[10]

As we argued in the previous chapter, the God revealed in Jesus is a nonviolent God. Such a God would not establish or ordain the institution of slavery, although this God would be aligned with the exposure of its violence and with the conditions of its collapse, as the powerful plantation owners are ejected from their thrones. The grain of the universe is visible in the womanist description of the Christian faith of slaves, whose suffering reveals the evil of the system of chattel slavery. And further, the grain of the universe, or in Martin Luther King Jr.'s image, the long arc of the universe that bends toward justice, is visible in the testimony to the power of God on the side of oppressed people, a power that discloses evil and exposes corruption.

Hermeneutics

In past times, African American churches developed a way of reading the Bible that white believers churches would do well to also cultivate. African Americans have a history of hearing the Bible speak with two voices. Slave masters quoted the Bible with a view to enforcing the obedience of their enslaved workers: "Slaves, obey your earthly masters with fear and trembling, in singleness of heart, as you obey Christ" (Eph 6:5). Owners emphasized that their enslaved workers should submit to suffering and beatings, following the example of Jesus' submission to suffering, beatings, and death. But the enslaved workers heard a different story from the Bible. They heard the story of the Israelites' escape from Egypt and from that story they learned that Israel's God was a God of liberation. When they heard the story of Jesus, they saw his resurrection as a victory over Satan and the forces of

---

10. See literature in previous note.

evil that created slavery, and understood that the liberator God of Israel was the God of Jesus, who brought liberation to oppressed people. Where the slavers had used Jesus to teach obedience and submission, the enslaved people heard the same story as a story of liberation.[11] And these elements are a central dimension of black theology today.

White peace churches would do well to learn from this double voiced hearing of the biblical story. The standard or dominant approach to the Bible has long appealed to Scripture to support the idea of a violent God who wreaks vengeance on enemies (as in the flood) or a controlling God who keeps order through the lethal violence of the state (i.e., the powers that be in Rom 13). In line with this conclusion, one voice in the Bible becomes a means of justifying the nation's wars as necessary to limit evil. In essence, the military forces of the nation are enlisted as God's enforcers.

This voice that proclaims God's violence is amplified by the conventional practice of many US presidents, who pronounce God's blessing on the nation's wars.[12] Continuing virtually to the present, the peace churches are not immune to a version of this justification, under the guise of two kingdom or perhaps two voice theology. In the peace church's voice, war is always wrong, but some times in the so-called real world, the other voice declares the necessity of the nation to wage war. But a church committed to nonviolence as followers of Jesus should read the Bible as he did, giving voice to the mercy and love of Israel's God. This God is most fully revealed in the birth, life, teachings, death, and resurrection of Jesus, who in his response to his enemies disclosed a God that rejects violence and blesses those who reject violence, even unto death on a cross. Such a story cannot be used to justify the nation's wars under any guise.[13] White peace churches would do well to learn this double-voiced reading of the Bible from African American churches: acknowledging the voice of violence and control while embracing the voice of peace and justice expressed in Jesus' life and teachings. In so doing, they would be aligning their exegesis with the grain of the

---

11. For example, Hopkins, *Shoes That Fit Our Feet*, ch. 1.

12. See Roosevelt, "D-Day Prayer." George H. W. Bush concluded his 1991 invasion of Iraq with these words: "Tonight, as our forces fight, they and their families are in our prayers. May God bless each and every one of them, and the coalition forces at our side in the Gulf, and may He continue to bless our nation, the United States of America." Bush, "Address to the Nation." George W. Bush claimed that God told him to invade Iraq. MacAskill, "George Bush: 'God Told Me.'"

13. For an evaluation and rejection of two-kingdom theology under any guise, see Weaver, "Living in the Reign of God."

universe—a reliable grain of love and truth and life amid recurring patterns of hatred and falsehood and death.

Theology

Another significant area for conversation is theology. And in the case of one of us (Denny), the fact of belonging to an Anabaptist tradition from which I inherited a sense of being a minority that stood outside or over against the dominant social order helped to prepare me to grasp theology from another tradition that was also not identified with the social order. In my first year of teaching in 1974 that sense of being different led me to ask whether there was a "Mennonite perspective" or a "Mennonite way" to teach about the standard doctrines of Christology, atonement, and Trinity. A version of that question remained with me throughout my entire teaching career. It evolved through many stages until reaching the current version: "What does theology look like that begins with and draws meaning from the narrative of Jesus?"[14] With this question, my first important theological focus was on atonement imagery.

As a result of asking questions about a "peace church perspective" or a nonviolent perspective on theology, I came to see that all versions of the dominant, satisfaction atonement paradigm required a God who used violence and who required and orchestrated the death of Jesus as the price of restoring order in God's universe. Accompanying this view of God was an image of Jesus as the obedient Son who patiently submitted to unjust violence because his Father required it—a problematic image for one steeped in the tradition, as I had learned as a small boy in Sunday school, of being like Jesus. In response, I constructed a nonviolent atonement image from the biblical narrative of Jesus that stressed victory over the forces of evil through the resurrection. I called this model "narrative Christus Victor" or more simply nonviolent atonement. As a corollary I also came to observe that the generic categories of "man" and "God" in the standard christological formulas of Nicea and Chalcedon allowed the church over the centuries to proclaim faith in Jesus Christ while espousing the sword that he rejected. This is because the standard christological formulas make no mention of the narrative of Jesus, which is where one discovers his rejection of the sword. Thus on the basis of a nonviolent atonement image constructed

---

14. In the not too distant future, I hope to produce an extended narrative about particular events and people that contributed to this evolutionary trajectory.

from the narrative of Jesus found in the Bible, I began to advocate a narrative approach to Christology as well.[15]

Once I had the beginning of an approach to an atonement motif and an approach to Christology that reflected a nonviolent perspective, I was curious to see what other distinctive theologies might say; that is, theologies that had a label to distinguish them from "standard" theology that appeared to have no label. I knew, for example, that black theology existed and that James H. Cone was a primary author of black theology. Without having any idea what I would find, I pulled Cone's *God of the Oppressed* off the shelf. What I found reoriented my entire theological agenda. Stated very briefly, what I discovered was that Cone offered a critique of satisfaction atonement imagery and of classic christological formulas parallel to my critique, except that where I had talked of accommodating or modeling violence, he wrote that classic christological terms accommodated slavery and racism, and that satisfaction atonement modeled slaves submitting to beatings and abuse. And parallel to my suggestion, Cone's beginning point for an alternative was the story of Jesus, whom he read as liberator, and understood in terms of a Christus Victor atonement motif with victory over evil in the resurrection.[16]

After reading Cone's observations, I realized that the question of violence in theology was much bigger than a Mennonite or peace church perspective. In fact, this question concerned the very foundation of all Christian theology. To give the import very succinctly, from Cone I saw that all theology and every theological statement reflects a particular context. Stated another way; every theology has a label, even when it is not named. Thus alongside a theology that reflected a peace church emphasis or black history, I could now see that the presumed general or standard theology should actually be labeled as white theology and violence-accommodating-theology. For example, as noted in the previous chapter, when the formulas from the Councils of Nicea or Chalcedon or the Cappadocians' trinitarian formula allow Christians to confess Jesus while wielding the sword or practicing the racism pointed out by James Cone, these statements would constitute white, violence-accommodating theology.

---

15. For my most complete statements of these two doctrinal complexes, see Weaver, *Nonviolent Atonement*, and Weaver, *Nonviolent God*. For a popular level version of these issues, see Weaver, *God Without Violence*.

16. See Cone, *God of the Oppressed*.

It then came as no surprise that womanist theologians—African American women doing theology—would reject the satisfaction atonement image. Early prominent womanist Delores Williams described the surrogacy of black women, namely the many abusive and oppressive roles that have been forced upon them: sexual surrogates for white masters while white women were considered delicate; doing field work that was men's work; caring for the white slave owner's children rather than their own, and more. After emancipation, black women worked as maids, caring for other people's children rather than their own; did the work of men who were humiliated or lynched. And they experienced discrimination both as women and as people of color. Williams wrote that to accept Jesus' suffering death as needed by God in satisfaction atonement was a theological validation of all this unjust surrogacy foisted on black women.[17]

Williams also offered a nuanced critique of black theology's focus on God as liberator. Williams wrote that the biblical figure of Hagar represents the experience of many black women. An Egyptian servant of Abraham's wife Sarah, Hagar was exploited by both a man and a woman. The first time, she was driven into the wilderness, God counseled her to return for her survival, and promised her son many descendants. The second time she was driven out, as a single mother she made a home for Ishmael. This is a story "in which a lone woman/mother struggles to hold the family together in spite of the poverty to which ruling class economics consign it. Hagar . . . goes into the wide world to make a living for herself and her child, with only God on her side." In a critique of black liberation theology, Williams then points out that the story of Hagar makes clear that the God of the Bible is not always a liberator. At times, God provides sustaining power in the midst of suffering and struggle.[18]

Recently, writings of J. Kameron Carter and Willie James Jennings have taken Cone's critique of the standard creedal formulas even further. Their work identifies the beginning of the accommodation of racism and the development of the idea of white supremacy in the separation of Jesus from his Jewishness by the early church fathers who developed the classic formulas. With Jesus separated from his Jewishness and the covenant with Israel, European theologians could then define Jesus as above racial identity, with European whiteness becoming the essence of what it meant to be human. Thus people of color became degrees of lesser human, and this theology

---

17. Williams, *Sisters in the Wilderness*, 162–67.
18. Williams, *Sisters in the Wilderness*, chs. 1, 6, quote 33.

was then used to justify European colonial domination and exploitation of peoples of color around the world who were deemed unable to properly care for or govern themselves.[19] Such work, alongside the work of Jewish biblical scholars like Daniel Boyarin and Amy-Jill Levine are a reminder to peace church theologians that the nonviolent way of Jesus Christ is not simply a New Testament story of peace that replaces the Old Testament story of violence. Rather, the merciful and nonviolent God of Jesus Christ is in fact the merciful and loving God of Israel—the God who freed the slaves and gave the law—summarized as the love of God and neighbor.

These observations lead us to suggest that there is much to discuss between theologians from the Anabaptist peace church and those of black and womanist theology. The goal of such a discussion is not to find one theology that fits both traditions. Since theology always emerges from and is shaped by a particular context, it is not even desirable to find a theology that would somehow account for the realities of both peace churches and black churches. However, there can and should be significant cross stimulation and much mutual learning from comparing experiences with so-called standard theology that has accommodated violence and racism. Potential discussions to pursue include such broad methodological issues as how critique develops, how questions arise and are pursued, how to reference the story of Jesus in making key theological claims, and more. Given the fact that this conversation is relatively new for white Anabaptists, they are the ones who have most to learn from this dialogue.[20] The goal of such conversations is not to achieve a new more authoritative synthesis of different theological perspectives but rather to align theological reflection with the grain of the universe that is visible in the story of Jesus and in the lives of those who bear crosses.

---

19. Carter, *Race*; Jennings, *Christian Imagination*.

20. In the interest of full disclosure, to my knowledge to date, I (Denny) am the only white, male, self-identified Anabaptist who has seriously engaged black and womanist theology. Alongside several articles, my most complete such discussions are the chapters on black and womanist theology in Weaver, *Nonviolent Atonement*, and sections of Weaver, *Nonviolent God*. Discussion of Carter and Jennings is in Weaver and Mast, "A Model in Conversation."

Additional Issues

Peace Theology and Practice

These comments on theology as a discipline open the door to other areas of potential discussion. There could be a specific conversation about peace theology, that is, the implications of Jesus' rejection of violence for Christians today. At least one predominantly African American church, the Church of God in Christ, had a pacifist beginning. In its constitution, this church still defines itself as "peace loving" and states that "the shedding of human blood or the taking of human life is contrary to the teaching of our Lord and Savior, Jesus Christ, and as a body, we are adverse to war in all its forms." Thus they reluctantly allow members to be inducted into the Armed Services, but insist that they serve only in "noncombatant units where we will not have to engage in acts of war or violence."[21]

Since the United States is not presently drafting young people into military service, perhaps more immediately profitable would be discussions about ways to protest injustice today. What does it mean to be a peace loving or nonviolent church living in the midst of systemic or structural racism; when the criminal justice system focuses more often and with steeper penalties on African Americans and other people of color than on white people who commit the same offenses; when social policies and tax structures burden the already poor while allowing money to accumulate with the already wealthy; when living in a society whose economy and foreign policy are increasingly oriented around perpetual war; and more? Conversations could deal with when, where, and how to engage in public protest, as well as other forms of resistance to injustice in this society. The following chapter has a more extensive discussion about active nonviolence, either to witness against these examples of systemic injustice or to make a more just alternative visible.

Church and State

The relationship of churches to the nation and its government poses ambiguities for both black and white believers churches. The state claims the highest loyalty of its citizens, but Christians also profess ultimate loyalty to

---

21. See the preamble to the constitution and the section on "War and Military Service," in Church of God in Christ, *Official Manual*.

Jesus Christ in whom God is revealed. How does a Christian decide which one to obey and which loyalty to compromise when the two claims come into conflict? For example, we suspect that nearly all Christians would recognize the right of governments to collect taxes, appealing for example to Jesus' words in Matt 22:21: "Give therefore to the emperor the things that are the emperor's, and to God the things that are God's." After all, tax money supports things that benefit all people, such as roads and bridges, public transportation, public schools, and much more. But for Christians opposed to war, taxes pose a problem since something approaching half of our tax money goes to pay for the military. Some people opposed to war keep their income intentionally low enough to avoid owing any taxes. Others withhold the percent of taxes owed that would go to the military, while many pay all their taxes. Meanwhile, African Americans pay taxes for services from which they have been and still are excluded.[22] What is the duty of Christian peacemakers in such cases, and what is an effective witness against tax monies misused?

Another dimension of church-state relations concerns the religious issues that the church may expect the state to enforce. There would appear to be no problem with establishing, for example, traffic rules that serve to allow all drivers to operate their vehicles in safety. Consequently, it is legitimate to expect that civil authorities will place some kind of sanction—usually fines—on those who break these rules. But some issues in the realm of ethics pose a different kind of problem, such as when the state is encouraged by Christians to enforce policies that are based primarily on religious belief. One such issue is abortion. Many Christians oppose abortion because of their conviction that abortion is a form of violence against human life created in the image of God, a stance typically labeled "pro-life." However, a large and vocal number of "pro-life" Christians seeks to enforce their convictions about the violence of abortion on the whole of American society by advocating for laws that restrict or ban abortion. Others who are pro-life seek rather to work for social policies that are likely to reduce the number of abortions—providing for comprehensive sexual education, making contraception more accessible, including family planning within insurance coverage, reducing the costs of health care, and advancing programs that

---

22. After WWII, African American veterans were excluded from much of the GI bill. See Weber, "How African American WWII Veterans." The interaction of African Americans with police is often different from that of white citizens. See Epp et. al., *Pulled Over*. Black farmers have had to fight the federal government to receive benefits denied them over a number of decades: See Brown, "Black Farmers to Receive Payouts."

address sexual and domestic abuse. A third group of Christians recognizes the problem of terminating potential human life and supports all the measures that would lessen the need for abortion, but also believes that harm is done to women by denying them the right to choose. These three stances on abortion are all found within the black community, religious or otherwise as much as in the white population, religious or secular.

In this context, banning abortion is an example of soliciting the state to enforce a particular religious belief on everyone—in this case a belief about the beginning of human life and the meaning of the act of terminating a pregnancy. In our society there is no consensus about the meaning of abortion; in fact, it is clearly one of the most divisive issues of our time. In our view banning abortion in our current context is an element of a de facto state religion as mentioned in a previous chapter (akin to requiring baptism of infants in the sixteenth century even for those who rejected it). The same analysis would apply to banning marriage of same sex couples or other elements of government policy that impact people who are LGBTQ. Thus an important element of conversation for both black and white believers church that are distinct from the social order would be how and when these churches expect the government to respect or enforce their particular religious beliefs.

Recognizing White Privilege

White people and people of color experience society differently in the United States. For the majority of white people, white is their dominant cultural experience. Most of their activities can take place with people who look like themselves. They do not have to feel out of place because they appear different from everyone else in a room or in a crowd. There is a white culture, actually multiple white cultures, but those who experience primarily these cultures do not recognize them as a culture. It is simply the way things are; it is their "normal" experience. Many white people thus live in a mono-cultural world. To live in these white cultures, with little learning about or being concerned about other cultures, is a bare bones description of white privilege.

In contrast, African Americans in the United States of necessity experience two cultures, their own and the white culture. In order to move smoothly through society, African Americans learn how to navigate white culture, which can differ greatly from their own. African Americans are thus of necessity multi-cultural.

A significant aspect of dialogue with black churches would be for white people to become better aware of their own culture. White people need to learn about white privilege. This means not only recognizing white privilege, but also coming to terms with the way that white culture exercises power to confer value, and defines beauty and knowledge. White privilege establishes a color hierarchy, with white at the top and people of color in lower and lesser ranks. Or as Drew Hart writes, "white" is a "category used to centralize power among a certain portion of humanity and at the direct harm and cost of people of color, especially Native American and black life in America."[23]

White privilege confers power on white people, even when they are oblivious to that power. Dealing with racism requires, among other things, acknowledging white power and being willing to confront it, or to use it to combat racism. For peace church Christians, addressing the harm caused by white privilege is akin to the work of conscientious objection. To refuse involvement in the system of war requires an understanding of how the war system works. As Nancy Bedford said, "Using the power of white privilege to confront racism is turning a sword into a plowshare."[24]

In this context, genuine dialogue requires learning about the experiences of black people in navigating this white culture, which devalues them but is still the dominant culture of the United States. Since black people already have awareness of white culture, white people clearly have the most to learn from this conversation. Meaningful dialogue should consist primarily of white Christians listening to African Americans talk about their experiences as people of color in the United States. This learning will include United States history and the way that racism has been largely erased from the standard accounts of American history, as well as current conditions and practices.[25] For white people, a crucial component of such learning is

23. Hart, *Trouble I've Seen*, 100–106, quote 101.
24. Bedford, "Narrow Gate?"
25. A good place to start is Loewen, *Lies My Teacher Told Me*, chs. 5, 6. For a detailed history of racism, see Kendi, *Stamped from the Beginning*. Debby Irving provides a description of growing up in unrecognized white privilege and her steps in learning to recognize it in *Waking Up White*. Books that document the difference between white and black people's encounter with the police are Alexander, *New Jim Crow* and Epp et al., *Pulled Over*.

the realization that one will never stop learning about racism and its impact on every person in the United States.

Dealing with Change

How the church responds to change might be a topic of fruitful dialogue. Anabaptists of various stripes and other believers churches over the years have dealt with the question of women in leadership. Already in the nineteenth century, a few of these churches had women in leadership positions. Through the twentieth century, there was much debate. Many changed their views and accepted women as leaders. Others still restrict ordained leadership roles to men. The processes occurred differently, but black churches have gone through the same stages, with many accepting women as ordained leaders and others still allowing only men to perform leadership roles. In all cases, these changes have involved both interpretation of Scripture as well as responses to pressure from wider American culture. We suggest that discussions of how change happens and how to respond to external stimuli could be mutually beneficial.

Perhaps more fraught is the question of people in the church community who are LGBTQ. Again for both white and black believers churches positions have ranged from exclusion to full inclusion in all functions of the church as well as the sanction of marriage between people with same gender affection. Some churches have maintained a consistent position of exclusion throughout the twentieth century and into the twentieth-first century. Others have changed radically in this regard, moving from exclusion to full inclusion. Again, we suggest that conversations about the use of the Bible and responding to the impact of societal pressures would be mutually instructive.

Conclusion

Conversations between black and white churches would benefit all participants. Since black people know more about white culture than whites know about black culture, it seems evident that white churches have the most to learn. Given the history of racism in this country, they have some catching up to do.[26] But establishing a true dialogue is not easy. It is not a matter of

---

26. This call for conversation between white and black churches mirrors Drew Hart's

chatting over coffee or at a church potluck. Genuine dialogue will require white people and white churches to get out of their white comfort zones and to spend time experiencing a minority community on its terms.

Alongside the mutual learning that will benefit the internal life of these churches there is an additional important reason for engaging in such dialogue. In 2016, a president was elected with significant support of white nationalists. That election result reveals an ongoing, noticeable racial divide and undercurrent of racism in American society. In this context, taking specific steps to engage in dialogue across racial lines would be a substantial witness in American society as a whole. The underlying racism and idea of white supremacy were there all along; the elected candidate in 2016 gave permission for it to become more visible. Thus the witness of a conversation across racial lines is important today, and will be for the foreseeable future. It is important for both the health of our churches and for our nation. And in that conversation, those who carry it out are indeed making visible the nonviolent justice-seeking grain of the universe.

---

invitation for dialogue. See Hart, *Trouble I've Seen*.

CHAPTER 6

Bearing Public Witness to the Gospel of Peace

IN THE MIDST OF the Reformation of the sixteenth century, Anabaptists set out in an ecclesiological direction new for that epoch. Although not without initial controversy, rejection of the sword, both of government and for personal self-defense, and a commitment to honesty in daily life, became identifying characteristics of this movement. This new nonviolent direction was grounded in the New Testament's story of Jesus and the early church, both of whom challenged the religious establishment and the empire from positions of relative social and cultural weakness—defenselessness. Among the implications of the nonviolent direction taken by early Anabaptism was an opening to faithful nonviolent action on behalf of social and economic justice and against the abusive and violent policies of modern states. While early Anabaptism had a quite visible public social witness, as documented in the dramatic narratives and vivid images of confrontation and protest found in the *Martyrs Mirror*, as a matter of survival Anabaptist communities like the Mennonites and the Amish eventually sought to avoid confrontation with authorities, seeking instead to build withdrawn communities of quiet witness that would not be seen as a threat to civil authority or established forms of Christianity. The Dordrecht Confession of Faith of 1632 makes this preference for flight over fight clear in its teaching on nonresistance: "From this we see that, according to the example, life, and doctrine of Christ, we are not to do wrong, or cause offense or vexation to anyone; but to seek the welfare and salvation of all men; also, if necessity should require it, to flee, for the Lord's sake, from one city or country to another, and suffer the spoiling of our goods, rather than give occasion for offense to anyone; and if we are struck on the right cheek, rather to turn the other also, rather than revenge ourselves, or return the blow."[1] This expression of traditional Amish and Mennonite nonresistance constitutes one valid way to understand the meaning of Jesus' teaching to love enemies, perhaps especially relevant for people who find themselves in vulnerable social locations. For example, this understanding certainly supports the practice of migration across borders of various kinds in order to find safety and security and to live in peace.

However, in a context like North America, where Mennonites and other peace church communities have established denominational networks with significant resources, and where peace churches have achieved some level of constitutional protection for their practices of conscientious objection to warfare, the practice of withdrawal and quietism can unfortunately be another way to enjoy the privileges of wealth and power while not really accepting responsibility for the harm perpetrated by such privilege. For example, some traditional Anabaptists are supportive of militaristic policies and capital punishment even though they would refuse to fight in a war or pull the switch for a gas chamber. Such a contradictory ethical posture is typically justified with some version of two-kingdom theology, which is one doctrinal support for a withdrawn alternative community. In this doctrine, it is the role of the state to wield the sword for justice and security, while it is the role of the church to proclaim the gospel and make disciples.

In 1950, a group of representatives from all of the major Mennonite groups ranging from the General Conference Mennonite Church to the Beachy Amish met in Winona Lake, Indiana, for a study conference on nonresistance and peace, during which the representatives approved a significant statement on peace as the will of God. In the aftermath of World War II, this statement challenged the withdrawn approach to nonresistance and peace by insisting that the way of peace is not just a special calling of the peace churches but God's will for all of humanity. For example, it stated that "we cannot be satisfied to retain for ourselves and our communities alone in any kind of self-centered and isolated enjoyment the great spiritual and material goods that God has bestowed upon us, but are bound in loving outreach to all to bear witness and to serve, summoning men everywhere to the life of full discipleship and to the pursuit of peace and love without limit."[2] This was a careful way of saying that God intends not just peace church people to refrain from war and violence, but all people, no matter what their station in life. Peace is God's will for all humanity. The

1. Van Braght, *Bloody Theater, or Martyrs Mirror*, 42.
2. Mennonite Central Committee, "Declaration."

Winona Lake statement therefore urged a movement beyond passive and withdrawn nonresistance toward a more socially-active form of witness. For example, it advocated for a Christian witness to the state: "We acknowledge our obligation to witness to the powers that be of the righteousness that God requires of all men, even in government."

Since that important 1950 study conference, North American Anabaptist churches have become increasingly involved in more activist expressions of witness to the state and to the surrounding social order. The range of communities that support such active witness includes the Bruderhof as well as churches that support the work of Christian Peacemaker Teams, although there has also been a reaction to such activism and a reassertion of the more traditional view of two-kingdom withdrawal among some Anabaptist churches as well. Moreover, since there has not been a military draft since 1973 in the United States, many Anabaptist churches have neglected to address their historic commitments to peace. Such neglect assumes a narrow view of the meaning of peace in the Anabaptist tradition—essentially not being required to join the military. Nevertheless, if we assume that peace is the will of God for all people—as the Winona Lake statement asserted—and if we understand the Word of God to be a real force for peace in the world—then we have both a mandate and a means for actively promoting the way of peace in our own time.

For example, in light of the ongoing and seemingly intractable persistence of racism and other forms of discrimination, along with the perpetual war stance that the United States has drifted into, it seems clear that nonviolent action on behalf of justice and peace is more relevant today than ever. Both the direction set by early Anabaptists and the story of Jesus provide precedents for the contemporary church as it seeks to live out the nonviolent Word, to work with and align with the grain of the universe. This chapter explores the basis for such nonviolent public witness to the justice and peace that God wills for the world and made visible in the life of Jesus.

In this discussion, nonviolence and nonviolent activism counter "violence." As "non" words, they are perhaps best understood in relationship to what they are not. The discussion to follow assumes a definition of violence developed by Glen H. Stassen and Michael L. Westmoreland-White. They understand violence as "destruction to a victim or victims by means that overpower the victim's consent."[3] This definition covers killing with weapons of all kinds, but it also includes the psychological harm caused by

---

3. Stassen and Westmoreland-White, "Defining Violence," 21.

systemic injustices of poverty, or discrimination on the basis of race or gender or sexual preference, or exploitative working conditions, or by bullying and negative stereotyping and belittling of children, sexual abuse, and more that could be listed. With this range of situations included under violence, not surprisingly nonviolence and nonviolent activism cover a wide variety of activities and approaches. In fact, they include all activities that expose injustice and violence and point toward justice and healing and restoration and ultimately to the reign of God made visible.

Anabaptists and Nonviolent Witness

In a number of ways, early Anabaptists were a visible witness to the word of Scripture and to Jesus the Word. The existence of the Anabaptist church itself was a witness. Baptism as the ritual of entry functioned as a visible marker for this church, and made clear that entry was open, regardless of social status, to any who professed faith in Jesus Christ and promised to live in obedience to his teachings. Baptism of adults followed the order of words attributed to Jesus in Matt 28:19, which first mentioned "making disciples" and then baptizing them.

Besides their practice of baptizing adults, a significant element of this visible witness of Anabaptists was rejection of the sword, along with a reputation for truthfulness and avoidance of an ostentatious life style. Such practices fit Anabaptists on the margins of society. The previous chapter expanded on those on the margins who bear crosses and thus whose witness aligns with the grain of the universe.

Of course, not all Anabaptists were pacifists. However, the debate among Anabaptists about rejection of the sword made that a defining issue in a way that was uncharacteristic of other Reformation era movements. Visible strands of Anabaptists who rejected the sword include the early Zurich group whose most well-known members were Felix Mantz and Conrad Grebel, the Schleitheim circle and Michael Sattler, Hans Denck, Pilgram Marpeck (see chapter 2 in this volume), Menno Simons (see chapter 3 in this volume), and Obbe and Dirk Phillips, as well as the Hutterites in Moravia.

The new movement produced visible excesses as well. One was the "naaktlopers," the infamous naked runners. In February 1535, a group of twelve radical Anabaptist men and women ran naked through the streets of Amsterdam to illustrate that "the truth is naked." They were arrested and subsequently beheaded.[4]

No doubt the greatest excess occurred in Münster. In actions that scandalized all of Europe, radical Anabaptists took over the city in 1534–35 and used the sword as the means to defend this visible manifestation of the kingdom of God—which included community of goods and polygamy. The city eventually fell to besieging Catholic forces and the defenders were massacred. In a challenge to the Münsterites, the Dutch Anabaptist faction of Obbe and Dirk Phillips and Menno Simons had opposed this violent Anabaptist manifestation from a pacifist direction. Menno's conversion constituted a visible nonviolent witness. He chose to join the pacifist faction of Dutch Anabaptists aligned with Obbe and Dirk in the immediate aftermath of the crushing of the scandalous occupation of Münster. This risky and courageous choice by Menno to identify with a despised religious minority led to a life of harassment by authorities, who sought to suppress Anabaptism, but was a striking, visible witness to what Menno called "true evangelical faith"; that is, a defenseless practice of the gospel that clothes the naked, feeds the hungry, comforts the sorrowful, shelters the destitute, returns good for evil, admonishes with the Word of God, and has become all things to all people.[5]

In addition to his writings on rejection of the sword, Pilgram Marpeck gave another kind of visible, nonviolent witness. Early in his career, he resigned or was removed from an important government position in Rattenberg and abandoned the city rather than participate in pursuing and executing Anabaptists. In Strasbourg he also pursued Anabaptist activities that led to his exile from the city.[6]

The ultimate visible witness of many early Anabaptists was martyrdom. The well-known *Martyrs Mirror* recounts many of these stories. Anabaptists considered their deaths to be a witness. That fact is clear from the numerous stories of Anabaptists singing or praying as they were led to the place of execution, and in the gruesome accounts of tongues being cut out to prevent such witnessing activity. This witness dimension of martyrdom is made clear in the longer title of *Martyrs Mirror*, which

---

4. See van der Zijpp, "Naaktlopers (Naaktloopers)." Perhaps one ought not stress "excess" in a judgmental way. Recall the account from Isa 20, which states that the prophet Isaiah walked naked and barefoot for three years to act out his foretelling that the king of Assyria would take the Egyptians and Ethiopians away as captives.

5. Menno, *Complete Writings*, 307.

6. Klaassen and Klassen, *Marpeck*.

includes the phrase "Bloody Theater."[7] But what is often missed in the reading of these martyr stories is that the Anabaptist witness recorded in the *Martyrs Mirror* includes far more than the moment of nonresistant death. This witness, as recorded in the *Martyrs Mirror* includes colorful accounts of Anabaptist protest against the unjust institutions and social arrangements of European Christendom, including numerous disputations with religious and civil authorities, clandestine meetings that included acts of civil disobedience such as adult baptism, and Simon the Shopkeeper's public refusal to kneel before a sacramental procession in the marketplace, to name a few.[8]

Simon den Kramer, Anno 1553.

Simon the Shopkeeper refusing to kneel.

The longer title of the *Martyrs Mirror* makes the dual commitment to defenselessness and a robust public witness visible: "The Bloody Theatre

---

7. Van Braght, *Bloody Theater; or, Martyrs Mirror*. For stories of witness and dismemberment, see throughout this volume.

8. For Simon the Shopkeeper's act of public protest against the civil religion of his time, see *Bloody Theater; or, Martyrs Mirror*, 540. Among the many accounts of Anabaptist disputations about matters of faith and life is the confession and witness of Jacques d'Auchy in *Bloody Theater; or, Martyrs Mirror*, 591–611.

PART TWO: ANABAPTISTS AND THE CONTEMPORARY BELIEVERS CHURCH

or the Martyrs Mirror of the Defenseless Christians." This makes clear that early Anabaptist pacifism was not a quietist form of nonresistance. The Anabaptists were indeed defenseless in that they accepted martyrdom rather than defend themselves with swords. But, in another sense, they were far from defenseless. They defended themselves with their witness to the Word, their verbal testimony to their faith, and the visible witness through the presence of their churches—which often engaged in acts of civil and religious protest.[9] In our contemporary image, this witness of martyrdom was carrying a cross that made visible the grain of the universe.

These multiple kinds of visible witness that are not defended with a sword can harken back to the New Testament's account of Jesus.

Jesus the Nonviolent Word[10]

Activism

When Jesus announced himself publicly in the synagogue at Nazareth, the mission had clear, visible social connotations. Quoting from Isaiah 61, he announced good news for poor people, release of captives, recovery of sight for people who are blind, and freedom for the oppressed (Luke 4:18). His ministry lived out and gave visibility to these promises.

In multiple ways, Jesus' teaching made visible the reign of God and contributed to the lived version of the nonviolent word. Parts of the Sermon on the Mount combined teaching and acting.

His words about turning the other cheek, giving coat with cloak and going the second mile have long been interpreted as an unrealistic ideal, a passive acquiescence to evil that would not work in the so-called real world. This interpretation follows the words in the King James Version, that "ye resist not evil" (Matt 5:38), language that is also reflected in most modern English translations of this text.[11] However, this time-honored interpretation does not capture the full picture of what Jesus seems to have

---

9. For a book-length, popular version of the origin of sixteenth-century Anabaptism, see Weaver, *Becoming Anabaptist*; and also Mast and Weaver, *Defenseless Christianity*, 15–71.

10. This section on actions and teachings of Jesus borrows from material in Weaver, *God Without Violence*, ch. 1, and Weaver, *Education with the Grain*, ch. 1.

11. For example, the New Revised Standard Version translates this text in a way that follows the King James Version: "But I say to you, Do not resist an evildoer" (Matt 5:38a)

been teaching about challenging wrongdoing. In fact, Jesus' commands are examples of nonviolent action in the face of injustice.

The phrase about not resisting an evil doer should actually be translated, "do not resist in kind" or "do not mirror evil."[12] The recent translation of the New Testament by David Bentley Hart, makes it more specific: "I tell you not to oppose the wicked man by force." Following this statement, Jesus then gave three examples of how to resist an evil doer without mirroring evil; that is, using violent force.

Matthew's version says to turn the other cheek after being struck on the "right cheek" (5:39). In that culture, the left hand was the unclean hand, and it was not used in public. Face someone and you will see that the only way to strike someone's right cheek with the right hand is with a back-handed slap. Thus this slap on the cheek is not intended to injure; its purpose is to insult, or to reinforce social inferiority. By turning the other cheek, the person slapped has refused the insult, and has left the slapper with two humiliating choices—either strike the open, left cheek with a right fist, which would acknowledge the person as an equal, or turn away humiliated. Even if the person slapped is later flogged, he or she has made an assertion of full humanity in the exchange.

The scene for the cloak and coat saying is debtors court. In Jesus' setting there was great shame in nakedness, but the shame fell not on the naked person but on the one causing the nakedness. Jesus' words picture a poor tenant farmer with impossible debt who faces the wealthy debt holder. The coat on the poor farmer's back is his only possession of value. And Jesus is saying in effect, when called on to give the coat for security in debtors court, take off your underwear as well and hand them to the debt holder. Standing naked and walking around naked the rest of the day will bring shame on the debt holder and the exploitative economic system. Again, this is a nonviolent action by which a person seemingly without power can gain the upper hand and expose an exploitative system.

The injunction about going the second mile constitutes a response to the Roman occupation of Palestine. Military rules of the occupiers gave a soldier permission at any time to commandeer a civilian and require him to carry the soldier's heavy, perhaps eighty-pound pack for one mile. But to lessen the anger of the locals, the soldier was forbidden to require the civilian to go more than one mile. Thus one who followed Jesus' suggestion and

---

12. This interpretation of this verse and of Jesus' three examples follows Wink, *Engaging the Powers*, 175–84, and Wink, *Jesus and Nonviolence*.

cheerfully carried a pack a second mile was actually placing the soldier in violation of his own regulations. Going the second mile reverses the roles. Rather than demanding that the civilian carry the pack, the soldier is now put in a position of begging the civilian to put it down before the soldier gets in trouble with his commander.

In these interpretations, Jesus was far from counseling passive submission—nonresistance—to evil. These three suggestions were actually examples of nonviolent actions in the face of provocation. He was suggesting positive but assertive ways that people without power could change a situation, witness against dehumanization and oppression, and give visibility to the full humanity to which all people are called by the reign of God.

The willingness to challenge the status quo displayed in these three suggestions is visible in other actions of Jesus as well. Luke 5:17–26 gives an account of healing a paralyzed man. In this familiar story, Jesus was teaching in a crowded house, and in order to get the man near Jesus, his friends let him down through a hole in the roof. But the detail of importance here is that upon seeing their faith, Jesus said, "Friend, your sins are forgiven you." A statement about forgiveness clearly scandalized the scribes and Pharisees, who complained that "God alone" can forgive. As the earthly manifestation of the reign of God, Jesus could most certainly offer forgiveness apart from the sacrificial system, a specific challenge to and witness against the orientation of the Pharisees.

The stories of healings by Jesus make visible the power of the reign of God that was present in him. One story in particular illustrates an additional point. Luke 6:6–11 reports on the healing of a "withered hand" on the Sabbath. His Sabbath actions were controversial, and Jesus knew that the authorities were watching to see if they could catch him in a Sabbath violation. He could have waited for the healing until the following day, as is pointed out in Luke 13:14 in an account of another Sabbath healing. But rather than waiting or being intimidated, Jesus called the man with the lame hand to come and stand by him. With the man highly visible, Jesus posed the question of whether it was lawful to do good or harm on the Sabbath. He then looked around at all of them (v. 10). In other words, he made eye contact and ensured that everyone there was watching. Only then did he command the man, "Stretch out your hand." On Jesus' part, this was a deliberate defiance and challenge of a restrictive rule. In today's language, it was an act of nonviolent activism. From another perspective, it was returning the Sabbath to its original purpose as a day of healing and restoration.

Jesus challenged barriers of race or ethnicity and of gender in visible ways. The Gospel of John 4:1–39 tells of a time Jesus traveled from Judea in the south to Galilee in the north of Palestine. This journey meant that he passed through Samaria. Antipathy between Jews and Samaritans was mutual. Actually being in Samaria was itself thus a remarkable event. According to the strict purity code, the Samaritans were of mixed ethnic heritage, which made them "unclean." Those who followed the strict law would not defile themselves by traveling in Samaria or interacting with Samaritans, which meant that Jesus' presence in Samaria was already a breach of the code. Then to compound this breach, when he stopped at the village of Sychar he asked a village woman for a drink of water. According to a strict interpretation of the purity code, a menstruating woman was considered unclean. Since one could not tell whether a woman was menstruating, men who observed the purity code would not touch a woman or a vessel that she had touched. When the disciples saw Jesus' interaction with this woman, they were greatly surprised. Not only was Jesus interacting with a Samaritan, it was a woman and he accepted a drink from her jar. While there are many levels of meaning that can be developed from this story, the point to draw out here is that Jesus took specific, visible steps to cross and challenge hurtful boundaries of race or ethnicity and gender.

Perhaps Jesus' most controversial act of challenge to the prevailing system was what by tradition has been called the "cleansing of the temple." The story is reported in all four Gospels (Matt 21:12–13; Mark 11:15–19; Luke 19:45–47; John 2:13–16). He entered the temple and began chasing out the animals being sold for sacrifices, and dumped over the tables of the money changers. John's account adds that he used a whip of cords in this action. Generally, he was telling them to take their unnecessary and corrupt practice out of the temple. It was a demonstrative cleansing of the temple. Today it would be characterized as assertive nonviolent action. This action arguably precipitated the plot by the authorities to have Jesus killed.

Since the action precipitated the fatal plot, it was clearly threatening to the class of people that ran the temple. The common assumption was that participating in a sacrifice was the way for individuals to find forgiveness and to be reconciled to God, and the priestly class enriched themselves greatly by selling the animals used in this practice. But Jesus was pronouncing sins forgiven without going through the process of a sacrifice. And by chasing the sacrificial animals and the money changers out of the temple, he was cleansing the temple of an unnecessary ritual and restoring it to its proper function. By demonstrating that sacrifices were unnecessary for forgiveness, Jesus definitely posed a threat to the priestly class. They wanted him eliminated. The protest cost him his life.[13]

On occasion, the temple cleansing has been used to argue that Jesus used violence. We are well aware that for those whose story includes a long history of brutal beatings (i.e., American slavery but also some nations today who use public whipping as a form of legal punishment), a whip in Jesus' hands does not sound like a nonviolent action. We suggest that we look at this action in the total scope of Jesus' life. At the beginning of his ministry, his announced mission in the synagogue was to bring good news to the poor, release of captives, sight to the blind, freedom for the oppressed (Luke 4:18). He taught love of enemies, responding to evil without mirroring it, and gave three examples of nonviolent resistance. The account of his life contains many acts of healing. These healings often contain statements of forgiveness. He forgave the woman taken in adultery. He broke Sabbath laws by healing on the Sabbath. His teachings and travel in Samaria confronted racism. Much more could be mentioned. At his trial, Jesus told Pilate, "My kingdom is not from this world. If my kingdom were from this world, my followers would be fighting to keep me from being handed over to the Jews. But as it is, my kingdom is not from here" (John 18:36). In other words, Jesus' kingdom had different standards than Pilate's violent kingdom. And finally there is the fact that Jesus did not use the action in the temple to initiate a violent rebellion, and the crucifixion of Jesus did not stimulate his followers to start a violent rebellion.

When considered in the full arc of Jesus' life, it seems clear that wielding a whip in the temple should not be considered an act of violence; it is not a departure from the character of practices and teaching visible throughout the duration of his career. The cracking whip is used to herd animals, not to injure people. This story is one more in the long arc of Jesus' life of vigorous, nonviolent protest or activism, an act of righteous indignation or even righteous anger. "My house shall be a house of prayer; but you have made it a den of robbers" (Luke 19:46). This particular action may have cost the money changers and the priests some money on that day. The equivalent today would be strikes and boycotts or other actions that cost the provider money until an injustice is corrected (i.e., the bus boycotts of the civil rights era or the current BDS movement that seeks

---

13. On the temple cleansing, see Crossan, *God and Empire*, 133–34, and Horsley, *Jesus and Empire*, 91–95.

to change policies of the Israeli state toward Palestinians living under occupation). In any event, none of the three synoptic accounts of the temple cleansing mention a whip and even John's account does not suggest that Jesus used the whip to hurt anyone.

Teaching

The assertive suggestions for dealing with an aggressor, challenging Sabbath rules and temple practices, and crossing ethnic and gender boundaries find an echo in some of Jesus' most well-known and/or confrontational teaching. When shown a coin with Caesar's image on it and asked whether it was lawful to pay taxes to Caesar, Jesus said, "Render to Caesar the things that are Caesar's and to God the things that are God's" (Luke 20:25). His opponents had hoped to trick Jesus into a dangerous admission, but his answer was not one with which they could find fault.

A lawyer from among the Pharisees asked Jesus which commandment was the greatest. Jesus' answer quoted from Deut 6:5 and Lev 19:18.

> You shall love the Lord your God with all your heart, and with all your soul, and with all your mind. This is the great and first commandment. And a second is like it. You shall love your neighbor as yourself.

On these two commands depend all the law and the prophets, Jesus added (Matt 22:36–38). In another version of this story, a lawyer asked Jesus what he needed to do to inherit eternal life. Jesus asked him what the law said, and the lawyer repeated these two commandments. Jesus replied that he was correct, that eternal life depended on these two commandments (Luke 10:25–28).

The scribes and Pharisees provide hard requirements of the law, Jesus said, but do not follow those laws themselves. Proclaiming "woe" on the scribes and Pharisees, he called them hypocrites and said that they go to great lengths to make a proselyte, but "then you make him twice as much a child of hell as yourselves." They make themselves appear very pious by tithing small things, such as herbs from the garden, but neglect more important parts of the law, such as "justice and mercy and faith." In their teaching of the law, they are like "blind guides! You strain out a gnat but swallow a camel!" This duplicity makes them like tombs, "whitewashed" on the outside to look beautiful, "but inside they are full of the bones of the dead and of all kinds of filth." Jesus had very sharp words about their references to the earlier prophets, who were persecuted. Although the scribes and Pharisees claimed that they would not have shed the blood of the prophets, Jesus accused them of doing exactly that in their own time. "You snakes, you brood of vipers! How can you escape being sentenced to hell?" Since such behavior invites retribution, Jesus laments the fate of the city. "O Jerusalem, Jerusalem, killing the prophets and stoning those who are sent to you. How often would I have gathered your children together as a hen gathers her brood under her wings, and you would not!" (quotes from Matt 23).[14]

The Reign of God Made Visible

This account of Jesus' actions and his confrontational teaching makes clear that the reign of God that Jesus represented was different from the society in which he lived. Stated differently, the reign of God challenged the injustices of Jesus' world, or the reign of God posed an alternative to the way things were. In a rule-centered context that prevented doing good on the Sabbath, Jesus returned the Sabbath to a day of healing and restoration. In a society where rules discriminated against ethnic minorities and identified women as second-class people, Jesus raised the status of women and racial and ethnic minorities. Followers of Jesus today will thus examine their host society in order to find ways to bring his story into the present, continuing his practices to bring healing and restoration and to witness against injustice and discrimination.

Jesus' action in the temple precipitated the plot to have him killed. As stated earlier, Jesus' comment before Pilate referred to the refusal to resort to violence in the reign of God. True to his statement, he submitted to crucifixion, and his followers did not use the moment to start an insurrection. In today's language, we might say that Jesus was a martyr for the reign of God. In any case, the God revealed in Jesus raised Jesus from the dead. This divine act was God's "seal of approval" on the life of Jesus as the presence of the reign of God, and the first fruits of what awaits all those who identify with the reign of God.

---

14. It is very important to make clear that with these strong words about the scribes and Pharisees, Jesus is not a proto-Christian separating himself from Judaism and opposing evil and corrupt Jews. He is rather acting as a Jewish prophet and teacher, critiquing and correcting his own tradition.

There is a precedent for nonviolent action and nonviolent struggle in the narrative of Jesus. But there is a profound theological validation as well. Christians profess that God is revealed in Jesus and in his story. This God is the Creator. If the character of the Creator God is revealed in Jesus, as we believe it is, then Jesus' rejection of violence and demonstration of nonviolent action reflect the nature of God and are an intrinsic dimension of the universe God created. As John Howard Yoder said, those who follow the nonviolent Jesus in bearing crosses "are working with the grain of the universe." Martin Luther King Jr. implied this same divine validation another way when he said, "The arc of the moral universe is long, but it bends toward justice."[15] Working with the nonviolent Jesus is to align oneself with a defining direction of the universe. This grain, this direction, becomes visible when we examine the world we live in through the lens of the story of Jesus.

This discussion of early Anabaptists and of the life of Jesus does not constitute a blueprint for twenty-first-century Anabaptists and other Christians to copy. Rather, they are important reference points in an ongoing story. The Christian story begins with Jesus, with the important caveat that the Christian story continues one that began with the Patriarch Abraham. Early Anabaptists are a historical movement, whose originating impulse was to build a church that expressed the story of Jesus. Today, we stand in this lineage. Our task is not to simply copy these forebears. Our task is to understand them in order to see the direction in which the story is moving and then to continue to move the story in the same direction in our own different context. Today, how do we give visibility to the grain of the universe and the long arc of justice?

The Visible Word Today: The Grain of the Universe

Neither Old nor New Testament provides a blueprint for the perfect economic system. What the Bible provides are criteria for evaluating attitudes toward wealth and the existing economic system. The system is just when even the most vulnerable people have access to the means to lead whole

---

15. Yoder, "Armaments and Eschatology," 58; King, "Where Do We Go from Here?," 199. With the idea that the character of the Creator God is revealed in Jesus' rejection of violence, it is worth recalling the discussion in a previous chapter of the conversation about divine violence in the Old Testament, with the story of Jesus indicating that the nonviolent side of the conversation best reflects the character of the God revealed in Jesus.

and healthy lives. For individuals, followers of Jesus give visibility to the reign of God—the grain of the universe—by gaining wealth honestly, by not seeking wealth for its own sake, by caring for the needy, and by living generously with wealth.

Neither Old nor New Testament provides a blueprint for a perfect political system. What the Bible provides are criteria for evaluating the existing political system. A just system protects the most vulnerable and those without clout, it looks out for the stranger—today's immigrants—and it does not discriminate on the basis of skin color or gender or ethnic origin or identity or form of love.

A seemingly obvious reference that covers both politics and economics is Matt 25:31–46. In this text, addressing all the nations, the Son of Man says that when food, drink, clothing and shelter were given to strangers and the needy, and when prisoners and the sick were visited, it was also done as to him.

The church witnesses to this text in many ways. Internal practices constitute a part of this witness. The rite of baptism joins people, regardless of status in society, into the body of Jesus Christ that is the visible witness to the world. Eating the bread and drinking the wine of communion acts out the practice of sharing goods and treasure. Decision making in which all voices are heard and valued is a model for a watching world.[16] Further, church structures such as Mennonite Central Committee and Mennonite Disaster Service both render service and serve as models of caring for those in need. Activities of the church in the local community, such as assisting programs for the homeless or for restorative justice or helping to settle refugees and immigrants, perform services reflected in the address by the Son of Man.

But situations arise that are not sufficiently addressed by these functions of the church. Regarding economics and political systems alone, all societies have issues to confront with regard to denial of justice for segments of the population. The question concerns how followers of Jesus should live and act so as to make the reign of God visible when faced with injustices. What happens when injustice exists in the status quo? How does the grain of the universe become visible in the face of discrimination of various kinds—against people of color or people without legal papers or refugees or Muslims or who are LGBTQ—or exploitative working conditions, and much more? How should contemporary Anabaptists continue the mission

---

16. Mast, *Go to Church*.

of Jesus to make the reign of God visible and to move society in the direction of alignment with the grain of the universe in the face of such entrenched conditions? Consider these options for dealing with problems, concerning both individual and then societal-wide or global examples.

For responses by individuals, consider first traditional Mennonite nonresistance, in which Christians refuse to respond to a provocation. They would willingly accept for themselves an assault or an injustice such as racial discrimination or low wages, since all forms of resistance and protest or strikes or union activity are considered to involve some level of violence. Passive nonresistance is an identifiable option that certainly fits within the framework of Jesus' teachings on loving enemies. But in many cases perhaps a more active response is warranted. When a response is needed, instead of a smart slap, perhaps a parent will give an aggressive child a short "time out" to reflect on his or her behavior. For a more serious offense, instead of a sound spanking, the parent may suspend play dates with friends for a few days. In terms of intruders, I (Denny) have collected several stories in which an intruder was confronted with kindness or offers of help, and the invasion was halted.[17] In today's drumbeat of reports of mass shootings at schools, churches, shopping malls, and other public spaces, we often miss the large number of shootings that were averted by nonviolent intervention, such as by throwing a harmless object like a basketball at the shooter to distract him or by engaging him in conversation. In fact, an FBI report on mass shooting incidents between 2000 and 2013 shows that in the vast majority of instances where civilians successfully disrupted a mass shooting, the civilian was unarmed.[18] Another approach is to study a martial art that teaches how to physically restrain an intruder without causing great bodily harm or death.[19] Notice that these examples form a continuum from least to most aggressive while always refraining from physical harm and lethal violence.

The United States appears to be in a state of perpetual war. Consider these responses to military or police violence. As a witness against war, some have written polite letters to the White House to suggest peaceful ways to deal with international conflict. Others have published sarcastic letters in their local news paper or have written letters to elected representatives with

---

17. For examples, see Willimon, "Bless You, Mrs. Degrafinried," and "Florida Women Disarm Intruder."

18. FBI, "Study of Active Shooter Incidents."

19. Thomas, "Martial Arts."

heated denunciations of war-like activity by the government. Some people have participated in public protests and demonstrations when organizers acquired a permit for such activity or as long as a permit on public property was not required. Others have protested without permits and have risked arrest through such activities as lunch counter sit-ins and library read ins and lie ins in congressional offices and die ins in public places to protest the shooting of unarmed black men by police officers. Others have blocked highway traffic or helped to occupy tribal sites to protect the lands of First Nations peoples from unwanted development. News media have reported on many such activities. In such highly visible actions, some have left when threatened with arrest, while others have submitted to arrest as a further witness against the injustice under protest. Still others have engaged in specifically illegal activity by cutting fences to enter or otherwise trespassing on military property to attempt to prevent the movement of military equipment or have even pounded on warheads to act out turning swords into plowshares. Again, notice that these examples are ranged from least to most assertive or confrontational but do not employ violence.

We can envision another list of activities that call attention to injustice inflicted disproportionately on people of color such as lead-laced drinking water or poor quality schools or police harassment. These activities might range from polite letters to hiring lawyers for legal suits to public marches to occupying mayoral or congressional offices to blocking traffic on major highways.

Such lists of activities both legal and illegal are by no means exhaustive. The limits on imagining such activities are confined only by the creativity of participants.[20] While we discuss examples of such creativity more extensively below, here we want to make a different point. It is possible to argue that each of these suggestions—and many more that could be added—are active ways to make visible in our world the nonviolent reign of God. Several even have parallels to actions of Jesus. For example, a polite letter or pointed meme on a social media platform might correspond to one of Jesus's comments such as "Render to Caesar what is Caesar's and to God what is God's." A sarcastic or forceful letter/meme might resonate with Jesus calling the Pharisees snakes or blind guides or beautiful white tombs filled with rotting flesh. Traveling through Samaria and interacting with a woman might be like a lunch counter sit-in during

---

20. Sharp, *Methods of Nonviolent Action*; Sharp, *Waging Nonviolent Struggle*; Ackerman and DuVall, *Force More Powerful*.

the Civil Rights Movement, while trespassing on a military base or illegally offering water and shelter to migrants crossing the border recalls healing on the Sabbath or the temple protest.

An important dimension of these examples is that they are arranged as a continuum of nonviolent activism, listed from least to most assertive or confrontational. No activity results in harm,[21] lethal danger or death to those confronted, although certainly there is a risk of harm to those who engage in such nonviolent confrontation. Eventually those who carry out the most assertive actions have submitted to fines and even imprisonment rather than to perpetrate physical harm or vengeance on people. These are continua of increasingly assertive nonviolent resistance, but resistance that does not injure or maim or kill people.

However, a common assumption often accompanies a list of such activities. The assumption is that the continuum contains additional steps. For example, past learning martial arts, an individual might buy a gun and take training in its use for self defense. A person concerned for violence in society might become a police officer with the intent to use a weapon infrequently. At a still wider level of concern for society, a person might join the National Guard, which deals with border security or domestic actions such as assisting with hurricane recovery. Another step on the continuum might be joining the military in a noncombatant capacity; then joining the military and accepting a combat role. Finally, at the extreme, one might join the military and prepare to use nuclear weapons.

Notice that for such additions to the continuum, the underlying assumption changes. It has become a continuum that describes the employment of increasing levels of violence.[22] When this set of options employing violence is assumed to be a natural continuation of the previous continuum of nonviolent actions, the character of the entire continuum changes. The very defining characteristic of the first half of the continuum shifts. It no longer contains examples of nonviolent resistance. Instead, all items listed are now assumed to exercise levels of violence, even gentle discipline of a child. It has become a continuum that measures the use of violence, from minimal

21. See below for discussion of loss of business revenue due to strike or boycott.

22. At this time, there is no universally recognized vocabulary for this discussion of violence and nonviolence. For example, in my (Denny) possession is a grid developed by Tim Peebles and Steve Thomas that develops a continuum of "Physical Force" that is parallel to my continuum of violence. Their grid includes "Action/Technique," "Intent/Purpose," and "Impact/Outcome" and is more detailed than space allows to discuss in this chapter.

to great. When confronted with this continuum, the question for peace people then becomes one of deciding how much violence they will tolerate, how much compromise with violence they will make in order to offer some challenge to injustice. Some defenders of redemptive violence make this application specifically. They argue that since we are already using violence in child discipline or in protests, we should recognize the positive contributions of some forms of violence, including on occasion military violence.[23] It has been common for conservative or traditional Mennonite churches to have this understanding of nonresistance. From this standpoint a professed commitment to complete nonresistance excludes the marches and protests and sit-ins of the civil rights movement and other movements for justice because they are considered exercises in violence—even if it is acknowledged that racial discrimination is sinful.[24]

It should be clear by now that we advocate a different distinction than the one made by the traditional Mennonite teaching between "resistance" and "nonresistance." We suggest instead that there are in fact two kinds of continua, those that assume the rejection of lethal harm and violence in the pursuit of justice and peace, and others that accept the use of violence, including lethal violence, for the sake of justice and peace. The first reflects efforts to make the reign of God visible in the face of injustice, while the second reflects "Pilate's kingdom" or the empire; that is, that rebellious part of reality that does not yet recognize the reign of God. The point that can mislead is that these two kinds of continua have one point in common—they intersect at the point of nonresistance. From that beginning point, however, they diverge in increasingly disparate directions.

As noted earlier in this chapter, Anabaptists constituted congregations that modeled nonviolent practices, including public confrontations with civil authorities, some of which got out of hand and crossed over into violence such as the takeover of Münster, but most of which were limited to verbal and symbolic forms of protest, such as Simons's provocative refusal to kneel during a public parade. Jesus taught in synagogues and on hill sides and he healed. He modeled acceptance by eating with those the religious establishment labeled "sinners." But he also challenged the status quo by healing on

---

23. For this argument in debate with my view, see Boersma, *Violence, Hospitality and the Cross*, 43–51; Boersma, "Violence, the Cross"; and Boersma, "Response to J. Denny Weaver."

24. J. Lawrence Burkholder shared this view that civil rights marches and protests exercised a level of violence, but called for compromising with this violence in order to do some good. See his discussion in Burkholder, "Limits of Perfection."

the Sabbath, forgiving sins, and traveling through Samaria and cleansing the temple. We can envision him suggesting lunch counter sit-ins and library read ins and bus boycotts and surrounding militarized police with bunches of flowers to stem police brutality or calmly occupying an office or business or public service to stop its discriminatory activity. We can imagine him urging his followers to break immigration laws in order to offer shelter, food, and water to migrants fleeing across the border for their lives.

This section has considered examples of witness to the grain of the universe that develop from the normal activity of the Anabaptist church. We also examined various examples of public, nonviolent protest, placed on a continuum of nonviolent resistance. Both witness and public protest find precedents in the story of Jesus as well as in the Anabaptist story. The point is that nonviolent action is not an aberration. Such action grows out of or is a continuation of the idea that Christians and the church pose a visible witness to the reign of God.

It is appropriate for contemporary Anabaptists to continue to exercise such nonviolent actions in our particular context. Our calling is not to copy these biblical and historical suggestions exactly, but rather to use them as a spur to think of actions that make sense in our contemporary setting. The possibilities are limited only by one's imagination.

Violence Within

There is a strong temptation to describe the efforts of the nonviolent church to confront evil and violence in the world in a dualistic way, as though the world outside the church is the only place such evil and violence exist. That temptation should be resisted because the assumption behind it is clearly wrong. The church has always been and continues to be a flawed and broken community that continues to betray.

That the church is flawed ought not surprise. It is composed of people, and people are flawed, even those who are committed to living within the story of Jesus. In fact, it has been flawed since the beginning—as is evident from the betrayal and abandonment of Jesus by the circle of disciples present at the Last Supper, as well as admonitions to his readers found throughout the writings of the Apostle Paul: "There is no one who is righteous, not even one" (Rom 3:10). What is called for, then, in our setting is the humility to recognize that the church is comprised of human beings who are prone to sin, and to live with a willingness to confess sin, accept correction, and to follow the practice of returning continually to the story of Jesus to ask again what it means and how to live within it. This process applies both to individuals who fail but also to communities and institutions of the church for which we have responsibility.

It is clear that even though they are committed to the way of peace, peace churches often have their own internal problems with violence, both systemic and physical. Here we speak particularly of Anabaptist churches as peace churches, and the ironical fact that the peace churches have often failed to live peacefully.[25]

Although stemming from a concern to take ethics seriously and to give a visible Christian witness, the peace churches have frequently failed to resolve their own conflicts without a rancorous parting. Anabaptist and Mennonite history contains many stories of conflicts that resulted in schisms and that left wounded feelings on all sides.[26] This pattern of unresolved conflict continues in the present over the struggle to include people who are LGBTQ in the life and leadership of congregations, conferences, and institutions of the Mennonite church. As LGBTQ advocacy groups work to change denominational and conference policies, along with traditional interpretations of Scripture, those who perceive a threat to the church's scriptural integrity respond by working to prevent such changes in the church's teachings and policies on sexuality and to exclude those who seek to change the policies. The outcomes of such conflict are often far from peaceable or nonviolent.

Another contemporary issue within the peace church concerns sexual abuse, especially of women and children—a problem that afflicts most Christian denominations including Anabaptist and peace churches.[27] At the forefront of this challenge is a disturbing history of actions by administrators and church officials to deal quietly with—that is, to cover up—abusive and harmful actions by men (and in a few cases, women) who engage in acts of sexual exploitation and violence in the context of church communities and institutions. Victims have been silenced or their stories suppressed in the name of protecting the reputation of institutions. As this is written, peace church leaders and institutions are only now starting to come to

---

25. For discussions of problems within the church and what can be learned from them, see Mast, "Why the Anabaptist Academy"; Heinzekehr, "Making Peace with Ourselves."

26. An excellent study of this tendency toward conflict in North American Mennonite communities is by Fred Kniss, *Disquiet in the Land*.

27. See Scarsella and Krehbiel, "Sexual Violence."

terms with these failures and continue in many instances to act in ways that give preference to protecting institutional structures over the lives of those who have experienced violence and hurt. In the context of these failures of the church to act rightly, movements for accountability and justice have sprung up that confront the church with its sins of abuse and neglect. One such organization—Into Account—provides support to survivors of sexual abuse in Anabaptist churches and communities by holding perpetrators and institutions accountable and advocating on behalf of survivors. Unfortunately, organizations like Into Account are often stigmatized as undermining the mission of the church because of the light that they are shining on the church's wrongdoing and thereby, it is assumed, harming the church's reputation. We see nonviolent action that challenges the church's violence and injustice in the same way that we see nonviolent action that challenges the violence and injustice of any social or political structure, including the state. Just as the prophets in the Hebrew Bible critique Israel and Judah, as well as the nations and empires that surrounded and threatened them, so should disciples of Jesus be committed to confronting violence and injustice wherever it appears. Indeed, Jesus was as critical of the religious establishment of his own people as he was of the Roman Empire that oppressed his community. Moreover, Jesus himself was not above criticism, as when he used a stereotype to address the Syrophoenician woman but then allowed himself to be corrected by her (Mark 7:24–30).

Some examples of nonviolent action organized to address the violence of the church against LGBTQ members within the context of our own denomination have ranged from passing out literature to wearing pink clothing or pink bracelets to singing between meetings to alternative worship services to guerrilla theater. These protests and actions within the church that call attention to experiences of exclusion faced by LGBTQ people have been a focal point of conflict, but that conflict has also contributed to the beginning of transformation in our denomination's relationship with its LGBTQ members.[28]

Protest as Invitation

At first level, protests and nonviolent actions confront and make visible a perceived injustice. In this instance it points to a wrong that needs to be

---

28. For more on Pink Menno's activism in Mennonite Church USA, see Mast, "Pink Menno's Pauline Rhetoric of Reconciliation."

corrected. The protest exposes an injustice. When this happens, it appears that those on one side are correct, and that those targeted by the protest are wrong. At this point, the nonviolent activism seems divisive. That observation is true as far as it goes.

However, a protest is more than a divide between good and evil, between righteous and unrighteous. A protest is also an invitation to repentance. A protest invites the perpetrators of injustice to recognize their fault and to repent, whichever side of the protest the perpetrators happen to be. In other words, participation in social protest is a step forward in acknowledging wrong, including the complicity of both the targets of protest and, at times, the protesters themselves. For example, a social action calling attention to climate injustice may be directed at, say, the harmful actions of a company that contributes excessive carbon to the atmosphere but the action may also help the protesters themselves repent of the large carbon footprint of their own lifestyles.

Jumping to reconciliation and peace without this step of acknowledgment and repentance allows injustice to stand. Thus protest is ultimately an invitation for perpetrators of wrong to cross over and join the side of justice. Recognition of wrong or injustice is the prerequisite to true reconciliation. At this level, nonviolent protest enables reconciliation. In the language used in part 1, the nonviolent Word is a disturbing and disruptive Word of God. But at the same time, this disruptive Word is also a reconciling Word.

Thus a protest contains within itself the potential to model the alternative. At it best, the protest makes justice, and ultimately the reign of God—the grain of the universe—visible in the face of the injustice being protested.

This movement has theological validation. The resurrection of Jesus, which is the divine validation that God was in the story of Jesus, poses an invitation for all to come and identify with Jesus and to live within the reign of God. To the extent that a protest makes visible the grain of the universe, to the extent that a person in the act of protest does so as a representative of the reign of God, to that degree the protest is a call for all involved to join in the effort to make visible and to experience the grain of the universe.

In Haiti in 1993 with a delegation sponsored by Christian Peacemaker Teams, I (Denny) experienced the grain of the universe—the reign of God—in a most direct way. Jean Bertrand Aristide, the popularly elected president of Haiti, had been ousted by a coup supported by the United States. Supporters of Aristide were in hiding. Our delegation's purpose in

Haiti was to give support and visibility to the plight of those in hiding. At the time in question, our group had formed a circle around the statue of a slave calling for rebellion, a statue that symbolized Haitian freedom. In one direction we faced military headquarter and turning ninety degrees we faced the government palace—the twin loci of power of the coup government. In our circle we sang and prayed for people in hiding and for the peace of Haiti. In the midst of this activity, I sensed an elderly gentleman at my right hand. When he had my attention, he simply said, "When I hear you praying, I have hope." This man had sensed that with our prayers and hymns, the reign of God—the grain of the universe—was tangibly present, and he had sensed and joined with it. I was overwhelmed. Never had I felt so close to the reign of God.

Again, the caution from the previous section is important. Those whose intent is to witness to the reign of God must do so with a sense that they also have something in common with the forces that are not aligned with the reign of God. This might be a silent alignment with the church that has perpetrated violence by ignoring the claims of women who were abused, or by suppressing people who identify as LGBTQ. Or from the previous chapter, it might involve people who identify with the minority status of the Anabaptist peace church, but then also identify with the white majority of United States society that has discriminated against people of color within as well as outside the church. And of course, these examples are by no means the only examples that could be named.

The important point here is that the invitation of the resurrection beckons all to examine themselves in light of the story of Jesus. This invitation includes those making protests as well as those who are the focus of protests.

Other Voices

Even as we say that it is the calling of Christians to make the reign of God visible, it is important to understand that the reign of God is not limited to the actions of Christians and the church. When the reign of God is visible in the grain of the universe, as we believe it is, it ought not surprise that individuals outside the explicitly Christian fold have sensed that grain as well, in actions both great and small.

Two names that come immediately to mind are the will-known Hindu Mohatma Gandhi and Muslim Khan Abdul Ghaffar Khan, called

Badshah Khan. Recall Khan's story from an earlier chapter. From Pakistan in the border region with Afghanistan, Khan came from a long tradition of vengeance killings, but came to realize that such killings only continued a cycle of violence. He swore himself to nonviolence, and raised a nonviolent force of 100,000 men that figured prominently in the struggle for Indian independence. Gandhi and Khan were close friends and lived and worked together during the independence struggle. Because of the effectiveness of Khan's movement, his nonviolent force experienced some of the worst violent repression by the British. Both Gandhi and Khan were bitterly disappointed when independence led to partition of Muslims from Hindus.[29] But certainly Gandhi and Khan sensed the grain of the universe.

A particularly touching and courageous story is the act by an anonymous Sinhalese woman in the midst of the 1977 anti-Tamil riots in Sri Lanka. A Tamil man had boarded a train in the town of Kandy. Sitting on the other side of the compartment he chose was a Sinhala woman. Riots had started in the town but he hoped the train would depart before they reached the station. But the train delayed, and rioters entered the train and were pulling Tamils out and beating them. There were cries of "Kill them!" As the rioters approached the Tamil man's compartment, the Sinhalese woman suddenly crossed over to sit by him, and held his hand, as though she were his wife. A rioter looked into the compartment and studied the situation. Leaving a Sinhalese woman a widow would be a serious act. He considered and then withdrew and passed the word, "No Tamils here. Go on to the next compartment." The train pulled out; the woman held his hand until her stop. She left the train, never having spoken a word.[30] This Sinhalese woman certainly sensed the grain of the universe.

Other examples of nonviolent struggle abound. Twelve chapters of the book *A Force More Powerful*, by Peter Ackerman and Jack DuVall, describe successful nonviolent struggles throughout the twentieth century. These accounts cover struggles in Europe and freedom movements around the world as well as the American Civil Rights movement.

Gene Sharp has written extensively on nonviolent action and struggle. His book *Waging Nonviolent Struggle* can serve as a one-volume primer.[31]

---

29. For Badshah Khan's story, see Easwaran, *Nonviolent Soldier of Islam*; and Pal, *"Islam" Means Peace*, 97–123.

30. This story is recounted in Daniel, *Charred Lullabies*, 211–12. It was called to our attention by Jonathan Larson.

31. Sharp, *Waging Nonviolent Struggle*. While Sharp's many writings comprise the largest body of theoretical writing on nonviolent activism, many women have

Sharp provides analysis of twenty-four cases of successful nonviolent struggle from the twentieth century. He organizes methods of nonviolent struggle in three categories: "protest and persuasion; noncooperation; nonviolent intervention," and provides a list that he calls "far from complete"[32] of 198 such methods.[33] Sharp's summary of methods describes

> protest marches, flying forbidden flags, massive rallies, vigils, social boycotts, economic boycotts, labor strikes, civil disobedience, boycott of phony elections, strikes by civil servants, sit-ins, hunger strikes, occupation of offices, and creation of a parallel government. Such methods may be used to protest symbolically, end cooperation, or disrupt the operation of the established system.[34]

The focus of nonviolent actions is not to destroy property. Exceptions are symbolic destructions, as pouring blood on draft records or burning draft cards during the Vietnam War. Fences have been cut to enter air bases to protest nuclear weapons. Other kinds of such destruction might include burning of flags and pictures, or pulling down of offensive statues. Not all advocates of nonviolent activism would engage in such acts. In contrast to riots or violent rebellions that destroy property and people, activist nonviolent responses that expose injustice can be maintained and sustained for long periods of time. They also point the way to reform and preserve lives and structures for a more just future.

Some will claim that nonviolent actions do cause at least monetary damage, as when a factory cannot produce goods because its workers are on strike, or restaurants and business lose revenue when they are boycotted because of refusing service to selected categories of people. But in our view, the protest actions are exposing injustice, and the lost revenue is what it costs the business to pursue an unjust policy. The loss of revenue is quickly stopped by adopting just practices. On the other hand, stopping the protests

---

participated in nonviolent activism and protests. Examples include Dorothy Day and Civil Rights activists such as Ella Baker, Septima Poinsette Clark, Fannie Lou Hamer, Bernice Johnson Reagon, Jo Ann Robinson, Coretta Scott King, and Rosa Parks, and the many womanist writers who have kept their names alive, such as Karen Baker-Fletcher, Katie Geneva Cannon, Kelly Brown Douglas, Cheryl A. Kirk-Duggan, Delores Williams, and Emilie Townes.

32. Sharp, *Waging Nonviolent Struggle*, 30.

33. For a definition of each method and examples of its use, see Sharp, *Methods of Nonviolent Action*.

34. Sharp, *Waging Nonviolent Struggle*, 49.

so that the businesses do not lose revenue is actually to ask the victims of discrimination to bear the costs of the unjust practices.

Nonviolent struggle is not for the faint of heart. Many of the actions described by Gene Sharp include civil disobedience and confronting police lines or military forces determined to protect the status quo. It takes courageous people to engage in nonviolent struggle. People have been seriously injured and killed practicing nonviolent resistance. Civil rights workers were murdered. Added to countless others, there are several examples with close ties to contemporary Anabaptists. During the war in Vietnam, Daniel Gerber went there on an assignment with Mennonite Central Committee. While working in a leprosarium, he was abducted by the Viet Cong and never seen again. Quaker Tom Fox was in Iraq with a delegation from Christian Peacemaker Teams. He was kidnapped; his body was eventually found on a garbage heap in March 2006. In March 2017, Mennonite Michael J. Sharp and a Swedish woman, Zaida Cafalan, were in the Congo on a United Nations mission to investigate human rights violations. They were kidnapped and went missing on March 12, 2017. Their bodies were found some days later in a shallow grave. That people may be harmed in nonviolent struggle is often raised as a critique. However, far fewer people are killed in nonviolent struggle than in violent resistance.

The first sections of this chapter sketched the biblical and theological basis for nonviolent activism. The vast majority of social movements for justice have been grounded in the life and resources of the church. From Quaker abolitionists and women's rights activists such as Lucretia Mott, Susan B. Anthony, and Alice Paul to the black Baptist tradition that gave rise to Martin Luther King Jr., many of the most prominent leaders and theorists of nonviolence have been grounded in the teachings of Jesus and became involved in social action as a matter of faith. We have also seen that commitment to nonviolence exceeds Christianity and a perspective of faith. For example, Mahatma Gandhi was influenced both by Christianity and Hindu mysticism. Badshah Khan was a Muslim. Moreover, many modern teachers and practitioners of nonviolence are motivated more by pragmatism than by theological commitments; for example, Peter Ackerman, Jack Duvall, and Gene Sharp.

Whether they are people of faith or not, many have advocated nonviolent struggle because it can work and has worked, and is a more effective means of confrontation and struggle than with arms and violence.[35] We

---

35. See parts 1, 3, and 4 of Sharp, *Waging Nonviolent Struggle*, and Ackerman and DuVall, *Force More Powerful*, 457–505.

add, it works because it reflects the grain of the universe, which becomes visible when we—Anabaptists, Christians—look at the world from the standpoint of the life and story of Jesus Christ. This observation does not separate the practice of nonviolence from a theological justification. On the contrary. It is on the basis of looking at the world through the lens of the story of Jesus that the idea of nonviolence becomes visible as an intrinsic element of the grain of the universe created by God.

CONCLUSION

The Grain of the Universe as Figure and Entanglement

IN THIS BOOK WE have explored early Anabaptist understandings of the "Word of God" as found in Scripture as well as in the church and the world. We have seen that Anabaptist writers and teachers from the early sixteenth century regarded the Word of God as both a creative power that grounds our being and a persistent force for changing our world—a defenseless capacity that intervenes from below, from a posture of weakness.

We have also explored how this vision of the Word of God as a transformative and defenseless power speaks to the church today beyond the Anabaptist tradition, offering a distinctive approach to reading Scripture that challenges the conventions of Protestant modernity, established during the Reformation era and its aftermath, and cemented during the modernist/fundamentalist conflict that raged for much of the twentieth century. As a result of that conflict, in modern Protestant practice, the Bible is regarded as either a revered textbook of inerrant data to be defended (fundamentalism) or a beautiful sourcebook of ancient myths to be problematized (modernism). Most Protestant interpretations of Scripture position themselves in relation to one of these defining models of meaning.

By contrast, when we follow an Anabaptist vision of the defenseless yet vindicated Word of God, the Bible is understood instead as a reliable guide to the life and teachings of Jesus Christ—the Word made flesh and the disarmed ruler of creation, depicted in John's apocalypse as the slain lamb who now occupies the throne (Rev 5:6–13). From this perspective, the Bible's value to the church is the gift of faithful vision—a capacity to see and follow the vulnerable and defenseless Word of God in the world today, to bear the cross and to inherit God's reign.

CONCLUSION: THE GRAIN OF THE UNIVERSE AS FIGURE AND ENTANGLEMENT

By using the word "defenseless" as a modifier, we are drawing on early Anabaptist terminology to highlight the vulnerability of the Word of God; we are not, of course suggesting the Word is passive. In early Anabaptist writings, the word "defenseless" (a translation of the German "wehrlos") characterized their refusal to defend themselves with armaments, as illustrated by the long title of the *Martyrs Mirror*, which says in part: "The Bloody Theater or Martyrs Mirror of the Defenseless Christians who baptized only upon confession of faith." To modern ears "defenseless" may sound passive but in the context of a book title that also includes the phrase "Bloody Theater," we can see that for early Anabaptists it was not. Anabaptists considered their defenseless deaths to be an active witness to their faith.

This Anabaptist vision of the Word of God as the life of Jesus Christ is not a new idea in the history of Christianity. It is as ancient as the first chapter of the Gospel of John and it is consistent with Trinitarian orthodoxy. And yet, in the context of the Protestant Reformation, Anabaptism advanced a distinctive teaching of the Word of God disarmed: noncoercive, defenseless, and not ours to defend. Michael Sattler put it quite succinctly in his speech to the magistrate during his trial: "You servants of God, I have not been sent to defend the Word of God in court."[1]

We have argued that this picture of the disarmed and defenseless Word advanced by early Anabaptism is consistent with the metaphor of the "grain of the universe" that is articulated in more recent Anabaptist theologizing, notably in the work of John Howard Yoder and Stanley Hauerwas. However, we should perhaps be clear here that we do not see the cross-bearing "grain of the universe" primarily as a new ground for apologetics or an entrée into natural theology, as explored by Stanley Hauerwas in his book *With the Grain of the Universe*. Hauerwas rightly exposes many of the modern projects to ground Christian truth in self-evident forms of natural law or order and proposes "the grain of the universe" as a fitting name for the wisdom of the cross that Christians are called to display in their lives.[2]

We are with Hauerwas in his description of the Christian life as bearing witness to the wisdom of the cross but we also see the defining feature of this wisdom more precisely: nonviolent love as the creative power that both grounds the cosmos and redeems its catastrophes. This creative power of nonviolent love is not passive or merely nice; by definition it constitutes a challenge to imperial or enslaving relations of power, to structures

---

1. Yoder, *Legacy of Michael Sattler*, 74.
2. Hauerwas, *With the Grain of the Universe*, 218–25.

CONCLUSION: THE GRAIN OF THE UNIVERSE AS FIGURE AND ENTANGLEMENT

of prejudice and supremacy that infect and corrupt life, including social and political life.

From the life and teachings of Jesus—indeed from his blessed mother Mary—we know that this power of creative and nonviolent love confronts both religious and political establishments that are based on status hierarchies and exploitative privilege. Surely, the incarnation of the Word brings down the powerful from their thrones and lifts up the lowly (Luke 1:52). Although it is nonviolent and loving beyond all else, the Word of God is more often than not experienced in human history as a disruptive and worrisome force when it makes an appearance—as was the case when Jesus of Nazareth appeared and began to preach the peaceable reign of God.

Sometimes this disruptive aspect of the mission of Jesus Christ is posed in a cynical way against the nonviolence he displayed, such as when the story of Jesus overturning the tables in the temple is offered as proof of Jesus' support of violence. And yet, as described in chapter 6, while this is certainly a story of institutional and marketplace disruption, there is no indication in any of the accounts of this public protest in the Synoptic Gospels that Jesus hurt anyone—even when he was driving the sheep and the cattle out of the temple courtyard with a whip of cords and pouring out the coins of the money changers (John 2:15–16).

This account of disruption in the temple cult found in John's gospel illustrates well how the Word of God as displayed in the life of Jesus Christ brings genuine peace by disrupting false peace. The Word of God brings peace—but this peace disrupts any "peace" that people make with violence or injustice or abuse both in the church and in the world. In other words, the Word exposes the false choice that political and institutional empires offer between violent action and passive peace. The Word shows the way to "doing something" without hurting someone.

We are not scientists but we view with curiosity and interest many of the emerging accounts of the basic structures of the physical universe as described in quantum theory. We believe that some of these discoveries vindicate the picture we have painted of the noncoercive yet reconciling actions of the Word of God.

For example, deterministic and controlling understandings of the universe are challenged by chaos theory, in which small events or variables within the initial conditions of a system can dramatically alter the system's development over time and across space—a phenomena known as the butterfly effect: a butterfly flapping its wings in the Amazon can impact the weather in China.

Quantum entanglement posits the relationship of particles in the universe that are light years distant from one another, a relationship that includes correlations of physical qualities such as motion and that is impacted by measurement and observation: that is, measuring the activity of a particle influences its properties. According to Brian Greene, the discovery of entanglement confirms that "the universe admits interconnections that are not local" and that vast space between two objects does not mean they are separate: "Something that happens over here can be entwined with something that happens over there even if nothing travels from here to there—and even if there isn't enough time for anything, even light, to travel between the events."[3] Quantum entanglement offers evidence of the attachment and communication that holds together the activity of vastly disparate objects, activity that Einstein called "spooky action at a distance." If we understand the universe in a mechanistic way, entanglement is indeed a bit spooky. From the perspective of the wisdom of the cross, however, none of this is surprising. The "grain of the universe" amplifies weak action, reconciles distant relationships, and confirms a deep attachment among cosmic bodies that transcends apparent order and predictability.

Quantum theory also invites us to take a less anxious view of entropy—the increasing disorder and unpredictability of a system—of our world and our lives, including our bodies. The second law of thermodynamics states that closed systems by nature's law always move toward disintegration and decay, toward less usable energy, toward what we experience as death. The reaction to this knowledge is often a controlling desire to fight entropy or to at least slow it down, to maintain order and hold off death.

However, physicist Carlo Rovelli proposes that we regard the increase in entropy as a force for life. The gift of low entropy—supplied in our case by the sun, or if we want to go back far enough, the big bang—keeps giving only because entropy increases, plants and animals grow, and systems become more complex: "The entire coming into being of the cosmos is a gradual process of disordering, like a pack of cards that begins in order and then becomes disordered through shuffling."[4] Rovelli gives the common example of a piece of wood that represents a system with fairly low entropy

3. Greene, *Fabric of the Cosmos*, 80.
4. Rovelli, *Order of Time*, 165.

until ignited by a flame that "opens a channel through which the wood can pass into a state of higher entropy."[5]

The example of fire and wood reminds us of the figurative association between fire and the Holy Spirit in Christian theology. Like fire or wind, we might posit, the Holy Spirit increases entropy and thus brings new life and new complexity. Yielding to the Holy Spirit is a way of yielding to life; perhaps in a way that explains how death is a condition for experiencing resurrection, how nonviolence is aligned with life and love, how people who bear crosses are working with the grain of the universe.[6]

To be clear, we are not arguing that death should be embraced as a kind of sacrificial offering to the hope of salvation—a conventional view that feminist philosopher Grace Jantzen has rightly critiqued in her brilliant account of Western visions of violence as intrinsic to salvation. Instead, with Jantzen, we see that entropy and death can be embraced as intrinsic qualities of natality—of the flourishing of creativity and life, rather than as tools of control and security.[7] Indeed, Jantzen's work helps us to see beauty and desire as instances of what we might call gifts of low entropy, given like the rays of the sun for the dispersion and birthing of new life and new love.

Finally, to return to one of the central themes of this book, we read the Bible to reflect the beauty and nonviolence of the Word of God displayed there. We see the Word of God alive in both sky and Scripture as a gift of low entropy and astonishing beauty that is then scattered like seed to both good soil and rocky ground, as depicted the parable of the sower (Matt 13:1–23). When we read the Bible with this story of indiscriminate and excessive dissemination in mind (considering again, perhaps, Menno's vision of the incorruptible seed), we are not surprised to find within the texts of the biblical canon a variety of responses to God's creative and nonviolent Word and to the creation that this Word spoke into existence.

Thus, when we read the Bible, we see both acceptance and rejection of the Word of God and we see the patience and persistence of the Word. We hear a diversity of voices both faithless and faithful to the Word. We see that when "the wicked draw the sword and bend their bows to bring down the poor and the needy, to kill those that walk uprightly, their sword shall enter their own heart, and their bows shall be broken" (Ps 37:14). We see violence

---

5. Rovelli, *Order of Time*, 162.
6. Yoder, "Armaments and Eschatology," 58.
7. Jantzen, *Violence to Eternity*, 196–200.

in the Bible; we find that the Word works against this violence from beginning to end, usually by deploying violence against itself.

When we read the Bible this way, we find that there is disagreement and disruption and disintegration, both in the stories of Israel and the church found in the Bible, and in the fragmentation of the text itself under the scrutiny of scholarship. The Bible's meaning can shift like the properties of a quantum particle under observation when we give it our attention. Nevertheless, when we read the Bible as the story of the human life and cosmic rule of Jesus Christ, we see that from Genesis to Revelation, "the LORD works vindication and justice for all who are oppressed" and that "the steadfast love of the LORD is from everlasting to everlasting" (Ps 103:6, 17).

The psalmist heralds a day when God will "speak peace to his people," a day when "steadfast love and faithfulness will meet, righteousness and peace will kiss each other" (Ps 85:8–10). According to the psalmist, the outcome of this cosmic kiss is that "faithfulness will spring up from the ground and righteousness will look down from the sky" (v. 11). This day has dawned, we believe, in the coming of Jesus Christ, who made visible for us the hidden and holy ways of the creator God—the one who from age to age gives life by speaking peace.

——— APPENDIX A ———

Anabaptist Lectionary

COMPILED BY
GERALD J. MAST

THIS LECTIONARY INTEGRATES IN a fifty-two-week cycle the following historic and contemporary Anabaptist (Swiss Brethren and Amish) lectionaries: Lectionary of the Münsterberg Congregation, Berne, Switzerland, 1763 (LM);[1] Lieder und Register von Kalona, Iowa, 1863–68 (LR);[2] *Schrift und Lieder*, Holmes County, Ohio, Amish Districts, 2009 (SL);[3] Raber's *Almanac*, 2017 (RA).[4] According to Donald Stoesz, this Swiss Anabaptist lectionary tradition was rooted in the Reformed Church adoption of a *lectio continua* approach that stresses a continuous reading of Scripture following the chapters and books in Scripture rather than thematic selections based in the church calendar—except for major feast days such as Christmas and Easter.[5]

---

1. Boldt, et al., *Mennonites in Transition*.

2. Byler, *Alte Schreibens*, 127.

3. *Schrift und Liede*. This publication collects all of the lectionaries used by Amish congregations in Holmes County and vicinity as of 2009. While they are all quite similar, I mostly relied on the lectionary associated with District 98, Fredericksburg East, on pp. 228–29. I selected this district because it happens to be the one led by my great grandfather Bishop Menno Mast during the mid-twentieth century. When I used other lectionaries from the SL, I identified those districts in the notes below.

4. *New American Almanac*, 48th ed., 2017. This annual publication issued by Raber's Bookstore prints a version of the Amish lectionary in an almanac style organized by the months of the year.

5. Stoesz, *Canadian Prairie Mennonite Ministers*, 68.

APPENDIX A: ANABAPTIST LECTIONARY

January	1. Matthew 2[6]	
	2. Matthew 3	
	3. Matthew 4	
	4. Matthew 5	(Sermon on the Mount)
February	5. Matthew 6	
	6. Matthew 7	
	7. Matthew 8	
	8. Matthew 9	
March	9. Matthew 10[7]	
	10. Matthew 11	
	11. Matthew 12	
	12. Matthew 14	
	13. Matthew 15	
April	14. Matthew 16	
	15. Matthew 13, John 15[8]	(Sower)
	16. Matthew 26, 27, 28[9]	(Easter)
	17. John 3, Romans 6[10]	(New Birth)
	18. Matthew 18, 1 Corinthians 5[11]	(Council/Preparation)

6. All the Anabaptist lectionaries follow Matthew 2–9 during the first two months of the New Year following Advent and Christmas.

7. Only LM does not include Matthew 10–12.

8. All the lectionaries combine Matthew 13 and John 15 as the "Saeman" (Sower) texts. This reading may appear either before or after Easter and Communion.

9. Amish lectionaries include only Matthew 26 and 27 as the Easter texts. A few of the Amish districts listed in SL do not include Matthew 26 and 27. Only the old Swiss Mennonite lectionary—LM—includes Matthew 28—the resurrection story.

10. The "Neugeburt" texts of John 3 and Romans 6 are common to Amish lectionaries but do not appear in the old Swiss LM.

11. All the lectionaries include Matthew 18 and 1 Corinthians 5 as the texts for "Ordnung" or council meeting / preparatory service before "Gros Gemein" or Communion.

APPENDIX A: ANABAPTIST LECTIONARY

May	19. Luke 22, 1 Corinthians 10–11, John 13: 1–18[12]	
		(Communion)
	20. John 8, Galatians 5[13]	(Freedom)
	21. John 17, 1 John 3 or Ephesians 4[14]	(High priestly prayer)
	22. Acts 1, 2[15]	(Pentecost)
June	23. Acts 3, 4[16]	
	24. Acts 5, 6	
	25. John 4, Revelation 14[17]	(Harvest)
	26. Acts 7, 8[18]	
	27. Acts 9, 10	
July	28. John 14, Romans 8 or Ephesians 5[19]	
	29. Luke 10, 1 Corinthians 13[20]	(Love)

12. Amish lectionaries all specify these particular verses to be read as Communion texts: Luke 22:1–33; 1 Cor 10:1–25; 1 Cor 11:2, 17–34; John 6:48–71; John 13:1–7 (or through 18 in some versions). The Swiss LM does not include these communion texts.

13. The "Freiheit" (Freedom) texts of John 8 and Galatians 5 appear either before or after Pentecost in the Amish lectionaries.

14. Jesus' high priestly prayer from John 17 appears in all Anabaptist lectionaries but is paired with a variety of other texts including the ones listed here: Romans 12 (RA), 1 John 3 (LM), 1 Thessalonians 5 (LR), Ephesians 4 (some districts in SL).

15. All Anabaptist lectionaries read Acts 1 and 2 for "Pfingsten" (Pentecost).

16. Anabaptist lectionaries vary in terms of how far they read into the book of Acts after Pentecost. LR goes all the way through Acts 6. RA and many of the lectionaries in SL go no further than Acts 1 and 2.

17. All Anabaptist lectionaries include John 4 and Revelation 14 as "Ernte" (Harvest) texts.

18. Only the Swiss LM includes Acts 7 to 10. These passages follow the "Ernte" texts of John 4 and Revelation 14 in the LM, as in this integrated lectionary.

19. Most Anabaptist lectionaries include John 14 (LM), but this text is paired with a variety of epistolary texts and its location varies in the lectionary cycle. RA includes it in mid-June and pairs it with it either Romans 8 or 1 Thessalonians 5. LR pairs John 14 with either Ephesians 4 or 5. District 6 in SL pairs John 14 with Ephesians 3.

20. The love chapter—1 Corinthians 13—is paired with a variety of texts in the Anabaptist lectionaries. RA pairs it with Luke 10. District 98 in SL pairs it with Colossians 3.

APPENDIX A: ANABAPTIST LECTIONARY

	30. John 16, Romans 12[21]	
	31. Luke 12, 13[22]	(Gathering)
August	32. Luke 14[23]	
	33. Luke 16	
	34. Luke 17	
	35. Luke 18	
September	36. Luke 19, Colossians 3	
	37. Luke 20	
	38. Hebrews 11[24]	(Old Testament Faithful)
	39. Hebrews 12	
	40. Hebrews 13[25]	
October	41. John 5, 1 Thessalonians 5[26]	
	42. John 9[27]	
	43. John 10, Ephesians 2[28]	
	44. Philippians 2[29]	

21. John 16 and Romans 12 appear together in the lectionary of District 5 in SL, following the Easter texts. John 16 is paired with Galatians 6 in District 9 or SL. Galatians 6 is also an optional pairing with John 16 for District 5 in SL. These texts do not appear in most Anabaptist lectionaries.

22. Luke 12 and 13 are listed as texts for "Einsammlung" (gathering) in most district lectionaries of SL. These texts appear in RA during mid-July.

23. Many Anabaptist lectionaries spend time in Luke during mid-summer. The Luke texts appearing here are selected from those texts that appear in at least some Anabaptist lectionaries.

24. All the Anabaptist lectionaries include Hebrews 11 and 12. RA lists Hebrews 11 and 12 in late October.

25. Hebrews 13 does not appear frequently in Anabaptist lectionaries but District 197 of SL pairs it with 1 Thessalonians 5.

26. John 5 appears in LM with 1 Thessalonians 5, but not in other lectionaries.

27. John 9 appears in LM paired with John 8.

28. John 10 is paired with Ephesians 2 in District 6's lectionary from SL.

29. In a rare appearance, Philippians 2 is paired with John 16 in District 197's lectionary from SL.

APPENDIX A: ANABAPTIST LECTIONARY

November	45. Matthew 20, 2 Corinthians 6[30]	
	46. James 2, 3[31]	
	47. James 4, 5[32]	
	48. Romans 13, 1 Peter 2[33]	(Worldly Authority)
December	49. Matthew 24[34]	(End of the World)
	50. Matthew 25	(End of the World)
	51. Luke 1[35]	
	52. Luke 2	(**Christmas**)

30. Matthew 20 is paired with 2 Corinthians 6 in many of the lectionaries in SL.

31. James 2 and 3 appear together in numerous lectionaries from SL and in late November in RA. These texts also appear in LR.

32. James 4 and 5 appear together in the lectionary of district 197 from SL.

33. Romans 13 and 1 Peter 2 frequently appear together in Amish lectionaries in the weeks leading up to Advent as "Obrigkeit" (Worldly Authority) texts.

34. All Anabaptist lectionaries include Matthew 24 and 25 at the beginning of the Advent season, identified as "Welt End" (end of the world) texts.

35. All Anabaptist lectionaries observe "Christag" (the Christmas season) with Luke 1 and 2.

—— APPENDIX B ——

Classic Trinitarian Terms in the *Martyrs Mirror*

J. Denny Weaver

THIS SHORT APPENDIX NOTES references to classic trinitarian terminology that appear in several accounts in the *Martyrs Mirror*. They display a persistent reluctance to use the standard categories, in particular the terms "person" and "Trinity." The preference of the Anabaptists is to use the language of scripture rather than terminology that came into use in later centuries. The usage displayed in this analysis constitutes additional evidence that the new churchly trajectory of Anabaptism had the potential to develop a distinct theological tradition. Following is a preliminary analysis.

In October 1559, while he was in prison awaiting his execution, Hans Vermeersch wrote out a confession that described his earlier interrogation. One paragraph dealt with his understanding of Father, Son, and Holy Ghost. He reports that he was asked if he believed in "God the Father, God the Son, God the Holy Ghost; three persons and one true God." Hans replied that he found only "one person" in the Scriptures, whom he identified as "Christ who was seen and heard." But he continues, no one has seen the Father nor the Holy Ghost. When asked whether he believed that there are "three persons," Hans replied, "No, unless it be shown me by the Scriptures." What he would accept is that they are "three in essence, yet only one true God. The Father is not the Son, nor the Son the Holy Ghost. The Father I confess as the Father; Jesus Christ as His Son who proceeded from Him; and the Holy Ghost, as proceeded from both the Father and the Son; yet, inseparably one true God." The reference given for this belief was John 17:8; 15:26.[1]

---

1. Van Braght, *Bloody Theater; or, Martyrs Mirror*, 632.

APPENDIX B: CLASSIC TRINITARIAN TERMS IN THE *MARTYRS MIRROR*

An extended letter from 1562 by Jelis Strings describes a conversation he had in prison with his opponents. Jelis initiated the part of the conversation related to Trinity by asking how the opponent "confessed the unity of God." The reply was "three persons and one God." Jelis then asked if the Holy Ghost were a "person," to which the answer was "yes." Jelis pointed out that if the Holy Ghost is a person, then one person can impregnate another as with Mary, while Acts says that when the Holy Ghost came to the apostles, he sat on each of them, although a person could sit on only one man. And the first chapter of the Book of Wisdom (Wis 1:7) says that the Spirit of the Lord filled the earth which a person could not do. Having set up what he considered a dilemma, Jelis asked to which person the opponent would compare the Holy Ghost, and he said that he did not know, and added that he did not consider them persons such as "Pieter, Klaes, and Jan." If they were not that kind of person, Jelis asked, to what could they be compared. After conferring with his companions, he replied that they only called them "persons," but clarified that for Jelis, person meant "human being." Jelis asked why call them persons, that is, human beings, when they were obviously not. When the opponent answered that "it amounts to the same thing," Jelis objected strongly, "A person is a human being, and you certainly cannot compare them to human beings." The opponent replied: "God the Father is not the Son; the Son is not the Father; the Holy Ghost is neither the Father nor the Son. And these are three; the one is what the other is not, and though they are three, yet are they but one God." And Jelis agreed: "This is also my faith, and in accordance with it I know but only one person, that is Jesus Christ, who was visible and palpable; but the others I do not know what to compare them to." On that point they agreed, and Jelis said that the opponent "let go his persons." Then the conversation turned elsewhere.[2]

Martyrs Mirror reports an extended disputation between Herman Vleckwijk, imprisoned in Bruges, and Friar Cornelis, which occurred on March 10, 1569. Comments on Trinity occur toward the middle of a fourteen-page transcript.

When Herman is accused of speaking "abominably of the holy Trinity," and asked whether he believes "Christ is the second person in the Godhead of the holy Trinity." Herman replied that "they know only to speak of things that are mentioned in the holy Scriptures." When pushed to acknowledge that the Scriptures speak of "God the father, and of God the Son, and of God the Holy Ghost," Herman responds that the Scriptures speak of "only one

---

2. Van Braght, *Bloody Theater; or, Martyrs Mirror*, 659–60.

APPENDIX B: CLASSIC TRINITARIAN TERMS IN THE *MARTYRS MIRROR*

God, and of the Son of the living God, and of the Holy Ghost." The friar then challenged Herman with the Athanasian Creed, which depicts three persons as one true God. Herman professes not to have studied the creed, because "it is enough for me, that I believe in the living God, and that Christ is the Son of the Living God, . . . and in the Holy Ghost, which is shed on us abundantly through Christ our Savior." The friar charges Anabaptists with following the accursed Erasmus as well as St. Hilary, who have written that in Scripture the Holy Ghost is nowhere called God. Herman responds that they follow neither Erasmus nor Hilary, "but we follow the Holy Scriptures, as Hilary and Erasmus herein do." Another exchange concerning Trinity concerns Herman's unwillingness to label Christ the man God, when "Christ, the second person in the Godhead or of the holy Trinity, became man." Herman's answer is that he calls "Him the Son of the living God, as Peter called Him (Matt.16.16), and Lord, as the apostles call Him."[3]

Pierijntgen Loosveldt was a forty-three-year-old woman arrested in 1572 in Flanders. Ten accusations were raised against her. Number seven questioned whether she would confess "that three persons constituted one true God." Her reply identified "three names in one Divine Being, namely Father, Son and Holy Ghost." But the Father who sent the Son she could not regard as a person because "the heaven is His throne, and the earth is His footstool," and also because Christ called the Father a Spirit. Neither could she understand the Holy Ghost as a person, who had sat on Christ in the form of a dove and on the apostles in the form of tongues of fire. But the Son, "who became man for us, was visible, palpable and passive," and walked among people displaying all manner of signs she could indeed "confess to be a person." The text supplies a number of scripture texts to support her comment.[4]

Well into the seventeenth century, Anabaptists were still suspect theologically. *Martyrs Mirror* reports on a confession of faith of October 8, 1626, which authorities in Holland required Anabaptists to make. After a century of Anabaptist development, this text reveals more theological acumen than the previous comments from persons who were not trained in theology, but the same intent to follow the Scripture rather than the received tradition is still evident.

The first section concerned "of the only God, Father, Son, and Holy Ghost." This article begins that according to the "testimony of the Word

---

3. Van Braght, *Bloody Theater; or, Martyrs Mirror*, 792–93.
4. Van Braght, *Bloody Theater; or, Martyrs Mirror*, 964.

of God, . . . there is one, only, eternal, almighty, merciful and just God." There follows a list of other attributes of the one God, all of which have scripture texts listed as proof. Following these attributes, the confession states that God also "makes Himself known in general by His Word," but also "distinctively and separately," as, "three that bear record in heaven." "Not three gods, but one Father, one Word or Son, and one Holy Ghost," which are made known in the baptismal formula. The Son proceeds from the Father "from eternity." The Father is not the Son, and the Son is not the Father. Likewise, the Holy Ghost is another that is not the Father, "But as far as the Father is God, eternal, uncreated, but the Creator of all things, . . . herein we believe that the Son and the Holy Ghost are one with the Father, to whom one and the same title of God, in the highest significance, honor, service, and obedience, belongs."

After this confession of three in one, these writers also stated that "the manner" of being three in one is not fully revealed, and that complete knowledge of it is not necessary for salvation. They doubt the wisdom of deep contemplation of this mystery above or beyond what they find in the Word of God. Thus "the terms of one essence, trinity, three persons, invented in former times by the ancients, we avoid, because they are unknown to the Scriptures, and because it is dangerous, in naming God, to use other words than those of the holy Scriptures."[5]

These several accounts of asserting the primacy of Scripture over the received tradition supply an additional indication that early Anabaptists began a new theological trajectory, befitting their new churchly trajectory, rather than simply adopting the theology of the church that they rejected.

---

5. Van Braght, *Bloody Theater; or, Martyrs Mirror*, 1107.

———— APPENDIX C ————

Anabaptist Use of the Apocrypha[1]

J. Denny Weaver

Many references to the Apocrypha are found in writings across the major Anabaptist traditions. The examples come from easily accessible sources, and this survey is by no means exhaustive.

In addition to Ecclesiastes and Proverbs, Menno Simons cites Sirach, also known as Ecclesiasticus or Ben Sira, when speaking of "the fear of the Lord" as the beginning of wisdom. He refers to Sirach when he counsels forgiveness and argues against seeking vengeance.[2] In fact, Sirach comes up frequently in Menno's writings, such as in his "Reply to Gellius Faber":

> Wherever the law is preached rightly and taken to heart so that it reveals its nature and power, there we find a broken spirit, a penitent, humble heart, and a conscience which trembles before the Word of its God, which checks and drives out sin, as Sirach says.[3]

Menno also quotes from 2 Esdras and Tobit.

Among Dutch Anabaptists, 2 Esdras 5:1–7 played an important role in the eschatological thinking of Melchoir Hoffman.[4] Menno's colleague Dirk Philips made frequent reference to the Apocrypha. The Scripture index to his collected writings covers more than a page and lists texts he cited from eleven different books of the Apocrypha. One example is Dirk's use of Wisdom of Solomon 2:23 and Sirach (also known as Ecclesiasticus) 17:3

---

1. This description of Anabaptist use of the Apocrypha first appeared in Weaver, *Education with the Grain*, 147–50.
2. Menno, *Complete Writings*, 949, 951, 1033.
3. Menno, *Complete Writings*, 717–18.
4. Williams and Mergal, *Spiritual and Anabaptist Writers*, 189n15

along with Genesis 1:26 and 5:1, and James 3:9 to state that human beings were created in the image of God.[5] David Joris, a member of another faction of Dutch Anabaptists, quotes from five apocryphal books.

The Froschauer Bible, which Swiss Anabaptists used, contains the Apocrypha. The letter by Conrad Grebel and his friends to Thomas Müntzer quotes the Apocrypha. Grebel included the twelfth chapter of Wisdom of Solomon in a list of Scripture texts that supported their belief that "all children who have not attained the knowledge to discern between good and evil and have not eaten of the tree of knowledge are surely saved through the suffering of Christ, the new Adam."[6] Balthasar Hubmaier made a significant use of the Apocrypha in his defense of free will. In his second tract on freedom of the will, he bases a two-page section on Ecclesiasticus 15, which says that the Lord placed the first humans in the garden with "free choice" (Sirach 15:14).[7] In one of two long citations from 4 Esdras (2 Esdras in modern numbering) in his letter from prison to his congregation at Horb, Michael Sattler uses that writer's words to encourage his congregation to be faithful to the end of the world. "Await your Shepherd, for He will give you the rest of eternity, for He is near, who will come at the end of the world; be ready for the recompense of the kingdom!"[8]

The South German and Moravian Anabaptists also made liberal use of the Apocrypha. In one passage, Hans Denck cited Sirach 27 along with Psalm 7 in an admonition to avoid "all selfish pursuits of this carnal life," and not to throw life away "as chaff to the wind." A bit later, he listed chapters 11 and 12 of Wisdom of Solomon along with biblical texts to say that God "gives everyone reason, grace and power to be transformed."[9] Pilgram Marpeck cited Judith 10:1–5 in a passage where he was emphasizing that it is not external appearances but the fruit of actions that determines their rightness. Judith had adorned herself "sumptuously," which could have been judged as "arrogance." However, since she used her appearance to gain entrance to the private chamber of Holophernes, the commanding general of Nebuchadnezzar's army, where she deceived and then

---

5. Dyck et al., *Writings of Dirk Philips*, 294.
6. Harder, *Sources of Swiss Anabaptism*, 290.
7. Hubmaier, *Balthasar Hubmaier*, 453–55.
8. Yoder, *Legacy of Michael Sattler*, 56, 62, quote from 2 Esdras 2:34–35, 62.
9. Liechty, *Early Anabaptist Spirituality*, 122, 123.

beheaded him, the defeat of this enemy of Israel displays the rightness of her sumptuous appearance.[10]

Hutterite leader Peter Walpot made used Sirach 13 as the basis for the admonition that before surrendering goods to the community, one should be firmly grounded in the truth, lest later one wish to have the goods returned.[11] Peter Riedemann referred to Wisdom of Solomon 13:1–3 and 15:14–19 in discussing the error of those who appropriate the material parts of God's creation for themselves rather than recognizing that all of God's creation is to be held communally. In another context, Riedemann included texts from 1 Maccabees 2, 3, 4, 5, and 6 in a long list of scriptures that show God's calling for revenge before it was abolished with the coming of Christ.[12] References to the Apocrypha are scattered throughout *The Chronicle of the Hutterian Brethren*. A section dealing with the second Great Persecution notes that "the prophet spoke the truth" when writing that there would be violent attacks on those that fear the Lord. This prophet was Ezra, quoted from 2 Esdras 16:70–75, followed by words of comfort quoted from Wisdom of Solomon 5:15–16. And the *Chronicle* writer can praise "the virtuous, praiseworthy Judith,"[13] mentioned above for Marpeck.

Last to be mentioned is the *Martyrs Mirror*, in which multiple citations appear from the Apocrypha. For example, Anna Jansz quoted 2 Esdras 7:6–9 in the letter she left to her son Isaiah before her martyrdom. In urging her son to follow the narrow but dangerous way of Christ, she used this text which described a city full of good things built on a plain, but approached only along a narrow path with fire on one side and deep water on the other. A man can never receive this city as an inheritance, Anna said, "if he never shall pass the danger set before" the city.[14]

In these examples, early Anabaptist writers cited texts from the Apocrypha alongside texts from what today is considered canonical Scripture. No distinction was made between the two. For these writers, the Apocrypha was Scripture.[15]

---

10. Marpeck, *Writings of Pilgram Marpeck*, 348.
11. Liechty, *Early Anabaptist Spirituality*, 188–89.
12. Riedemann, *Peter Riedemann's Hutterite Confession*, 119–20, 221–22.
13. *Chronicle of the Hutterian Brethren*, 312, 756.
14. Van Braght, *Bloody Theater; or, Martyrs Mirror*, 453.
15. For a recent article that supports this conclusion, see Seiling, "Solae (Quae?) Scripturae."

APPENDIX D

Hymn by Michael Schneider

TRANSLATED AND VERSIFIED BY
Gerald J. Mast

O Lord God ruling from your throne
EIN FESTE BURG   87. 87. 66. 66. 7

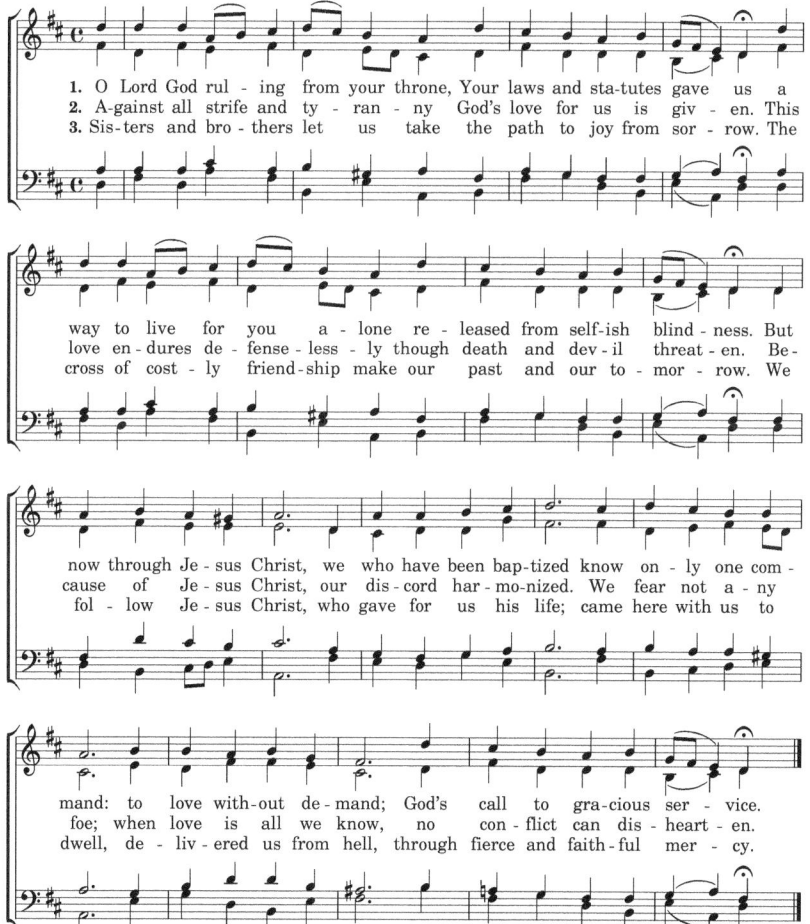

1. O Lord God rul-ing from your throne, Your laws and sta-tutes gave us a way to live for you a-lone re-leased from self-ish blind-ness. But now through Je-sus Christ, we who have been bap-tized know on-ly one com-mand: to love with-out de-mand; God's call to gra-cious ser-vice.

2. A-gainst all strife and ty-ran-ny God's love for us is giv-en. This love en-dures de-fense-less-ly though death and dev-il threat-en. Be-cause of Je-sus Christ, our dis-cord har-mo-nized. We fear not a-ny foe; when love is all we know, no con-flict can dis-heart-en.

3. Sis-ters and bro-thers let us take the path to joy from sor-row. The cross of cost-ly friend-ship make our past and our to-mor-row. We fol-low Je-sus Christ, who gave for us his life; came here with us to dwell, de-liv-ered us from hell, through fierce and faith-ful mer-cy.

Text: Michael Schneider, "O Herre Gott in deinem Thron," *Ausbund,* 1564; tr. Gerald J. Mast, 2017
Music: Martin Luther, 1529, *Geistliche Lieder,* 1529, 1531

Bibliography

Ackerman, Peter, and Jack DuVall. *A Force More Powerful: A Century of Nonviolent Conflict*. New York: Palgrave, 2000.
Ahlstrom, Sydney E. *A Religious History of the American People*. New Haven: Yale University Press, 1972.
Alexander, Michelle. *The New Jim Crow: Mass Incarceration in the Age of Colorblindness*. Rev. ed. Foreword by Cornel West. New York: New Press, 2012.
Allen, James. *Without Sanctuary: Lynching Photography in America*. Santa Fe, NM: Twin Palms, 2000.
Ausbund, das ist: etliche schöne christenliche Lieder . . . Basel: von Mechel, 1838.
Baker-Fletcher, Karen. *Dancing with God: The Trinity from a Womanist Perspective*. St. Louis: Chalice, 2006.
Barth, Karl. *Church Dogmatics*. I.2, *The Doctrine of the Word of God*. Edinburgh: T. & T. Clark, 1956.
Bauman, Clarence, trans. *The Spiritual Legacy of Hans Denck*. Leiden: Brill, 1991.
Bedford, Nancy. "A Narrow Gate? Proceeding by the Spirit along the Way of Jesus." Keynote address, Word, Spirit and the Renewal of the Church: Believers' Church, Ecumenical and Global Perspectives, Goshen College, 2017.
Beecher, Henry Ward. "The Tendencies of American Progress." In *God's New Israel: Religious Interpretations of American Destiny*, edited by Conrad Cherry, 235–48. Rev. ed. Chapel Hill: University of North Carolina Press, 1998.
Beecher, Lyman. "On Disestablishment in Connecticut." In *Church and State in American History*, edited by John F. Wilson, 92–93. Boston: D.C. Heath, 1965.
———. "A Plea for the West." In *God's New Israel: Religious Interpretations of American Destiny*, edited by Conrad Cherry, 12–30. Chapel Hill: University of North Carolina Press, 1998.
Biesecker-Mast, Gerald. *Separation and the Sword in Anabaptist Persuasion: Radical Confessional Rhetoric from Schleitheim to Dordrecht*. C. Henry Smith Series 6. Telford, PA: Cascadia, 2006.
———. "Spiritual Knowledge, Carnal Obedience, and Anabaptist Discipleship." *Mennonite Quarterly Review* 71 (1997) 201–26.
Blough, Neal. *Christ in Our Midst: Incarnation, Church and Discipleship in the Theology of Pilgram Marpeck*. Kitchener, ON: Pandora, 2007.
Boersma, Hans. "Response to J. Denny Weaver." In *Atonement and Violence: A Theological Conversation*, edited by John Sanders, 33–36. Nashville: Abingdon, 2006.

———. *Violence, Hospitality and the Cross: Reappropriating the Atonement Tradition.* Grand Rapids: Baker, 2004.

———. "Violence, the Cross, and Divine Intentionality: A Modified Reformed View." In *Atonement and Violence: A Theological Conversation*, edited by John Sanders, 47–69. Nashville: Abingdon, 2006.

Boldt, Andrea, et al., eds. *Mennonites in Transition from Switzerland to America: Emigrant and Immigrant Experience*, Anabaptist Documents, 37–55. Morgantown, PA: Masthof, 1997.

Boyarin, Daniel. *Border Lines: The Partition of Judaeo-Christianity.* Philadelphia: University of Pennsylvania Press, 2004.

Boyd, Gregory A. *The Crucifixion of the Warrior God.* Vol. 2. Minneapolis: Fortress, 2017.

Brown, Carolyn M. "Black Farmers to Receive Payouts in $1.2 Billion from Federal Lawsuit." *Black Enterprise*, October 2, 2013. https://www.blackenterprise.com/black-farmers-to-receive-payouts-in-1-2-billion-from-federal-lawsuit-settlement/.

Burkhart, Irvin E. "Menno Simons on the Incarnation (Continued)." *Mennonite Quarterly Review* 4 (1930) 178–207.

——— "Note: Menno Simons on the Incarnation (a Correction)." *Mennonite Quarterly Review* 6 (1932) 122–23.

Burkholder, J. Lawrence. "The Limits of Perfection: Autobiographical Reflections." In *The Limits of Perfection: A Conversation with J. Lawrence Burkholder*, edited by Rodney J. Sawatsky and Scott Holland, 1–54. 2nd ed. Waterloo, ON: Institute of Anabaptist and Mennonite Studies, Conrad Grebel College, and Pandora, 1993.

Bush, George H. W. "Address to the Nation on the Invasion of Iraq." *American Rhetoric: Online Speech Bank.* January 16, 1991. https://www.americanrhetoric.com/speeches/ghwbushiraqinvasion.htm.

Byler, John M, ed. *Alte Schreibens.* Amish Documents and Records Series. Sugarcreek, OH: Schlabach, 2008.

Cannon, Katie Geneva. "'The Wounds of Jesus': Justification of Goodness in the Face of Manifold Evil." In *Katie's Canon: Womanism and the Black Soul of the Community*, 101–12. New York: Continuum, 1995.

Carter, J. Kameron. *Race: A Theological Account.* New York: Oxford University Press, 2008.

Church of God in Christ. *Official Manual.* Memphis, TN: Church of God in Christ, Inc., 1991. http://cogicjustice.net/wp-content/uploads/2012/04/COGIC-OFFICIAL-MANUAL.pdf.

Cone, James H. *The Cross and the Lynching Tree.* Maryknoll: Orbis, 2011.

———. *God of the Oppressed.* Rev. ed. Maryknoll: Orbis, 1997.

Cooper, Derek, and Martin L. Lohrmann, eds. *Reformation Commentary on Scripture.* Old Testament 5. Downers Grove: InterVarsity, 2016.

Crossan, John Dominic. *God and Empire: Jesus against Rome, Then and Now.* San Francisco: HarperSanFrancisco, 2007.

Daniel, E. Valentine. *Charred Lullabies: Chapters in an Anthropology of Violence.* Princeton, NJ: Princeton University Press, 1996.

Denck, Hans. *Schriften.* Vol. 2, *Religiöse Schriften.* Edited by Walter Fellmann. Quellen Zur Geschichte der Täufer 6. Gütersloh, Germany: Bertelsmann, 1956.

Dyck, Cornelius J., et al., trans. and eds. *The Writings of Dirk Philips, 1504–1568.* Classics of the Radical Reformation 6. Scottdale, PA: Herald, 1992.

Easwaran, Eknath. *Nonviolent Soldier of Islam: Badshah Khan, a Man to Match His Mountains.* Tomales, CA: Nilgiri, 1999.

Eisenstein, Elizabeth L. *The Printing Revolution in Early Modern Europe*. Cambridge: Cambridge University Press, 1993.

Epp, Charles R., et al. *Pulled Over: How Police Stops Define Race and Citizenship*. Chicago: University of Chicago Press, 2014.

Erb, Abe, ed. *Schrift und Lieder*. Sugarcreek, OH: Carlisle, 2009.

FBI. "A Study of Active Shooter Incidents in the United States Between 2000 and 2013." https://www.fbi.gov/file-repository/active-shooter-study-2000-2013-1.pdf/view.

Finger, Thomas N. "Confessions of Faith in the Anabaptist/Mennonite Tradition." *Mennonite Quarterly Review* 76 (2002) 277–97.

———. *A Contemporary Anabaptist Theology*. Downers Grove: InterVarsity, 2004.

"Florida Women Disarm Intruder with Food, Rum." *Dayton Daily News*, October 31, 2003.

Fountain, John W. "No Fare: You're Black. You're Male. You Just Want a Cab. Why Is It So Cold Out There?" *Washington Post*, May 4, 1997.

Friesen, Abraham. *Erasmus, the Anabaptists, and the Great Commission*. Grand Rapids: Eerdmans, 1998.

Froschouer, Christoffel. *Die ganze Bibelm, neue Auflage*. Denver, PA: Hoover, 1975.

Greene, Brian. *The Fabric of the Cosmos*. New York: Vintage, 2005.

Gregory, Brad. *Salvation at Stake: Christian Martyrdom in Early Modern Europe*. Cambridge: Harvard University Press, 1999.

Grislis, Egil. "The Doctrine of the Incarnation according to Menno Simons." *Journal of Mennonite Studies* 8 (1990) 16–33.

Harder, Leland, ed. *The Sources of Swiss Anabaptism: The Grebel Letters and Related Documents*. Classics of the Radical Reformation 4. Scottdale, PA: Herald, 1985.

Hart, David Bentley. *The New Testament: A Translation*. New Haven, CT: Yale University Press, 2019.

Hart, Drew G. I. "Salvaging Mennonite Theological Education: Imitating Black Theology as It Imitates Christ." In *Education with the Grain of the Universe*, edited by J. Denny Weaver, 74–86. C. Henry Smith Series 11. Telford, PA: Cascadia, 2017.

———. *Trouble I've Seen: Changing the Way the Church Views Racism*. Harrisonburg, Va.: Herald, 2016.

Hauerwas, Stanley. *With the Grain of the Universe: The Church's Witness and Natural Theology*. Grand Rapids: Brazos, 2001.

Hege, Christian, et al. "Pappenheim, Marschalk von." In *Mennonite Encyclopedia*, edited by Harold Bender et al., 4:115–16. Scottdale, PA: Herald, 1959.

Heinzekehr, Hannah E. "Making Peace with Ourselves: Mennonite Peace Education and Intrachurch Conflict." In *Education with the Grain of the Universe*, edited by J. Denny Weaver, 155–63. C. Henry Smith Series 11. Telford, PA: Cascadia, 2017.

Hopkins, Dwight N. *Shoes That Fit Our Feet: Sources for a Constructive Black Theology*. Maryknoll: Orbis, 1993.

Horsley, Richard A. *Jesus and Empire: The Kingdom of God and the New World Order*. Minneapolis: Fortress, 2003.

Hubmaier, Balthasar. *Balthasar Hubmaier: Theologian of Anabaptism*. Translated and edited by H. Wayne Pipkin and John H. Yoder. Classics of the Reformation 5. Scottdale, PA: Herald, 1989.

Hut, Hans. "On the Mystery of Baptism." In *Early Anabaptist Spirituality: Selected Writings*, edited and translated by Daniel Liechty, 64–81. Classics of Western Spirituality. Mahwah, NJ: Paulist, 1994.

Hutterian Brethren, ed. and trans. *The Chronicle of the Hutterian Brethren*. Vol. 1. Rifton, NY: Plough, 1987.

Hymnal: A Worship Book. Elgin: Brethren, 1992.

Irving, Debby. *Waking Up White and Finding Myself in the Story of Race*. Cambridge, MA: Elephant Room, 2014.

Irwin, Joyce. "Embryology and Incarnation: A Sixteenth-Century Debate." *Sixteenth-Century Journal* 9 (1978) 93–104.

Jantzen, Grace M. *Becoming Divine: Towards a Feminist Philosophy of Religion*. Bloomington: Indiana University Press, 1999.

———. *Power, Gender, and Christian Mysticism*. Cambridge: Cambridge University Press, 1995.

———. *Violence to Eternity*. New York: Routledge, 2009.

Jennings, Willie James. *The Christian Imagination: Theology and the Origins of Race*. New Haven, CT: Yale University Press, 2010.

Kaufman, Gordon D. *In Face of Mystery: A Constructive Theology*. Cambridge: Harvard University Press, 1993.

———. *Jesus and Creativity*. Minneapolis: Fortress, 2006.

Keeney, William E. *The Development of Dutch Anabaptist Thought and Practice from 1559–1564*. Nieuwkoop, Netherlands: De Graff, 1968.

———. "The Incarnation, a Central Theological Concept." In *A Legacy of Faith: The Heritage of Menno Simons*, 55–68. Newton, KS: Faith and Life, 1962.

Kendi, Ibram X. *Stamped from the Beginning: The Definitive History of Racist Ideas in America*. New York: Nation, 2016.

King, Martin Luther, Jr. "Where Do We Go from Here?" In *A Call to Conscience: The Landmark Speeches of Dr. Martin Luther King, Jr.*, edited by Clayborne Carson and Kris Shepard, 165–99. New York: Warner, 2001.

Kirk-Duggan, Cheryl A. "African-American Spirituals: Confronting and Exorcising Evil through Song." In *A Troubling in My Soul: Womanist Perspectives on Evil and Suffering*, edited by Emilie M. Townes, 150–71. Bishop Henry McNeal Turner Series 8. Maryknoll: Orbis, 1993.

Klaassen, Walter, and William Klassen. *Marpeck: A Life of Dissent and Conformity*. Scottdale, PA: Herald, 2008.

Kniss, Fred. *Disquiet in the Land: Cultural Conflict in American Mennonite Communities*. New Brunswick, NJ: Rutgers University Press, 1997.

Krahn, Cornelius. "Incarnation of Christ." In *Mennonite Encyclopedia*, edited by Harold Bender et al., 3:18–20. Scottdale, PA: Herald, 1959.

———. "Menno Simons." In *Mennonite Encyclopedia*, edited by Harold Bender et al., 3:577–84. Scottdale, PA: Herald, 1959.

Konkel, August. *1 & 2 Chronicles*. Believers Church Bible Commentary 30. Harrisonburg, VA: Herald, 2016.

Levine, Amy-Jill, *Short Stories by Jesus*. New York: HarperCollins, 2014.

Liechty, Daniel, trans. and ed. *Early Anabaptist Spirituality*. New York: Paulist, 1994.

Loewen, James W. *Lies My Teacher Told Me: Everything Your American History Textbook Got Wrong*. New York: Simon & Schuster, 1995.

MacAskill, Ewen. "George Bush: 'God Told Me to End the Tyranny in Iraq.'" *Guardian*, October 7, 2005. https://www.theguardian.com/world/2005/oct/07/iraq.usa.

Marpeck, Pilgram. "Exposé of the Babylonian Whore." Translated and introduced by Walter Klaassen, in Klaassen et al., *Later Writings by Pilgram Marpeck and His Circle*, 19–48.

———. *Later Writings by Pilgram Marpeck and His Circle*. Vol. 1, *The Exposé, A Dialogue, and Marpeck's Response to Caspar Schwenckfeld*. Translated by Walter Klaassen et al. Kitchener, ON: Pandora, 1999.

———. "Pilgram Marpeck's *Response* to Caspar Schwenckfeld's *Judgement*." Translated and introduced by John Rempel, in Klaassen et al., *Later Writings by Pilgram Marpeck and His Circle*, 1:67–157.

———. *The Writings of Pilgram Marpeck*. Translated and edited by William Klassen and Walter Klaassen. Scottdale, PA, Herald, 1978.

Martin, Clarice J. "Biblical Theodicy and Black Women's Spiritual Autobiography: 'The Miry Bog, the Desolate Pit, a New Song in My Mouth.'" In *A Troubling in My Soul: Womanist Perspectives on Evil and Suffering*, edited by Emilie M. Townes, 13–36. Bishop Henry McNeal Turner Series 8. Maryknoll: Orbis, 1993.

Martin, Dennis. "Menno and Augustine on the Body of Christ." *Fides et Historia* 20 (1988) 41–64.

Mast, Gerald J. *Go to Church, Change the World: Christian Community as Calling*. Harrisonburg, VA: Herald, 2012.

———. Jesus' Flesh and the Faithful Church in the Theological Rhetoric of Menno Simons." In *The Work of Jesus Christ in Anabaptist Perspective: Essays in Honor of J. Denny Weaver*, edited by Alain Epp Weaver and Gerald J. Mast, 173–90. Telford, PA: Cascadia, 2008.

———. "Pink Menno's Pauline Rhetoric of Reconciliation." *Pink Menno*, August 2, 2013. http://www.pinkmenno.org/2013/08/pink-mennos-paulines-rhetoric-of-reconciliation/.

———. "Suffering Mission in the Passau Songs of the Ausbund." *Anabaptist Witness* 4 (2017) 15–35.

———. "Why the Anabaptist Academy Should Go to Church." In *Education with the Grain of the Universe*, edited by J. Denny Weaver, 181–93. C. Henry Smith Series 11. Telford, PA: Cascadia, 2017.

Mast, Gerald J., and J. Denny Weaver. *Defenseless Christianity: Anabaptism for a Nonviolent Church*. Telford, PA: Cascadia, 2009.

McIntosh, Peggy. "White Privilege: Unpacking the Invisible Knapsack." *Peace and Freedom*, July/August 1989, 10–12.

Mennonite Central Committee. "Declaration of Christian Faith and Commitment." 1950.

Menno Simons. *The Complete Writings of Menno Simons*. Translated by Leonard Verduin. Scottdale, PA; Herald, 1956.

———. *Opera omnia theologica, of alle de godtgeleerde wercken van Menno Symons*. Amsterdam, 1681.

Nelson-Pallmyer, Jack. *Jesus Against Christianity: Reclaiming the Missing Jesus*. Harrisburg, PA: Trinity, 2001.

Oosterban, J. A. "The Theology of Menno Simons." *Mennonite Quarterly Review* 35 (1961) 187–96, 237.

Ozment, Steven. *Protestants: The Birth of a Revolution*. New York: Doubleday, 1992.

Packull, Werner O. "Pilgram Marpeck: Uncovering of the Babylonian Whore and Other Anonymous Anabaptist Tracts." *Mennonite Quarterly Review* 67 (1993) 351–55.

Pal, Amitabh. *"Islam" Means Peace: Understanding the Muslim Principle of Nonviolence Today*. Santa Barbara, CA: Praeger, 2011.

Pelikan, Jaroslav. *The Reformation of the Bible: The Bible of the Reformation.* New Haven, CT: Yale University Press, 1996.

Rempel, John D. "Critically Appropriating Tradition: Pilgram Marpeck's Experiments in Corrective Theologizing." *Mennonite Quarterly Review* 85 (2011) 59–75.

———, ed. and trans. *Jörg Maler's Kunstbuch: Writings of the Pilgram Marpeck Circle.* Kitchener, ON: Pandora, 2010.

———. *The Lord's Supper in Anabaptism: A Study in the Christology of Balthasar Hubmaier, Pilgram Marpeck, and Dirk Philips.* Studies in Anabaptist and Mennonite History 33. Scottdale, PA: Herald, 1993.

Riedemann, Peter. *Peter Riedemann's Hutterite Confession of Faith.* Translated by John J. Friesen. Scottdale, PA: Herald, 1999.

Rivera, Mayra. *Poetics of the Flesh.* Durham, NC: Duke University Press, 2015.

Roosevelt, Franklin D. "D-Day Prayer." *The History Place: Great Speeches Collection.* http://www.historyplace.com/speeches/fdr-prayer.htm.

Rovelli, Carlo. *The Order of Time.* New York: Riverhead, 2018.

Scarsella, Hilary Jerome, and Stephanie Krehbiel. "Sexual Violence: Christian Theological Legacies and Responsibilities." *Religion Compass* 13 (2019). https://doi.org/10.1111/rec3.12337.

Schaff, Philip, ed. *The Evangelical Protestant Creeds.* 6th ed. Grand Rapids: Baker, 1983.

Seibert, Eric A. *Disturbing Divine Behavior.* Minneapolis: Fortress, 2009.

Seiling, Jonathan. "Solae (Quae?) Scripturae: Anabaptists and the Apocrypha." *Mennonite Quarterly Review* 80 (2006) 5–34.

Sharp, Gene. *The Methods of Nonviolent Action.* Politics of Nonviolent Action 2. Boston: Porter Sargent, 1973.

———. *Waging Nonviolent Struggle: 20th Century Practice and 21st Century Potential.* N.p.: Porter Sargent, 2005.

Sider, Ronald J. *The Scandal of the Evangelical Conscience.* Grand Rapids: Baker, 2005.

Smith, H. Shelton, et al. *American Christianity: An Historical Interpretation with Representative Documents.* New York: Scribner, 1963.

Snyder, C. Arnold, ed. *Later Writings of the Swiss Anabaptists, 1529–1592.* Translated by Harold S. Bender et al. Anabaptist Texts in Translation 6. Kitchner, ON: Pandora, 2017.

Sprunger, Keith L. "Dutch Anabaptists and the Telling of Martyr Stories." *Mennonite Quarterly Review* 80 (2006) 149–82.

Stassen, Glen H., and Michael L. Westmoreland-White. "Defining Violence and Nonviolence." In *Teaching Peace*, edited by J. Denny Weaver and Gerald Biesecker-Mast, 17–36. Lanham, MD: Rowman and Littlefield, 2003.

Stoesz, Donald. *Canadian Prairie Mennonite Ministers' Use of Scripture: 1874–1977.* Victoria, BC: Friesen, 2018.

Terrell, JoAnne Marie. *Power in the Blood? The Cross in African American Experience.* Bishop Henry McNeal Turner / Sojourner Truth Series in Black Religion 15. Maryknoll: Orbis, 1998.

Thomas, Steve. "Martial Arts as a Model for Nonviolence: Resisting Interpersonal Violence with Assertive Force." *Conrad Grebel Review* 33 (2013) 72–91.

Van Braght, Thieleman J., ed. *The Bloody Theater; or, Martyrs Mirror.* Translated by Joseph F. Sohm. Scottdale, PA: Herald, 1987.

Van Der Zijpp, Nanne. "Naaktlopers (Naaktloopers)." In *Mennonite Encyclopedia*, edited by Harold Bender et al., 3:804. Scottdale, PA: Herald, 1959.

Vanhoozer, Kevin J. *Biblical Authority after Babel: Retrieving the Solas in the Spirit of Mere Protestant Christianity*. Grand Rapids: Brazos, 2016.

Voolstra, Sjouke. *Het Woord Is vlees geworden: De melchioritisch-menniste incarnatieleer*. Kampen: Uitgeversmaatschappij J. H. Kok, 1982.

———. *Menno Simons: His Image and Message*. Edited by John D. Thiessen. North Newton, KS: Bethel College, 1996.

Walpot, Peter. "True Yieldedness and the Christian Community of Goods." In *Early Anabaptist Spirituality: Selected Writings*, edited and translated by Daniel Liechty, 138–96. Classics of Western Spirituality. Mahwah, NJ: Paulist, 1994.

Weaver, J. Denny, ed. *Education with the Grain of the Universe*. C. Henry Smith Series 11. Telford, PA: Cascadia, 2017.

———. *God Without Violence: Following a Nonviolent God in a Violent World*. Eugene, OR: Cascade, 2016.

———. "Living in the Reign of God in the 'Real World': Getting beyond Two-Kingdom Theology." In *Exiles in the Empire*, edited by Nathan E. Yoder and Carol A. Scheppard, 173–93. Studies in the Believers Church Tradition 5. Kitchener, ON: Pandora, 2006.

———. *The Nonviolent Atonement*. 2nd ed. Grand Rapids: Eerdmans, 2011.

———. *The Nonviolent God*. Grand Rapids: Eerdmans, 2013.

Weaver, J. Denny, and Gerald Biesecker-Mast, eds. *Teaching Peace: Nonviolence and the Liberal Arts*. Lanham, MD: Rowman and Littlefield, 2003.

Weaver, J. Denny, and Gerald J. Mast. "A Model in Conversation with Black and Evangelical Theology." In *John Howard Yoder: Radical Theologian*, edited by J. Denny Weaver, 294–333. Eugene, OR: Cascade, 2014.

Weber, Brandon. "How African American WWII Veterans Were Scorned by the G.I. Bill." *Progressive*, November 10, 2017. https://progressive.org/dispatches/how-african-american-wwii-veterans-were-scorned-by-the-g-i-b/.

Wengert, Timothy, ed. *The Roots of Reform*. Vol. 1 of *The Annotated Luther*. Minneapolis: Fortress, 2015.

Williams, Delores S. *Sisters in the Wilderness: The Challenge of Womanist God-Talk*. Maryknoll: Orbis, 1993.

Williams, George H., and Angel M. Mergal, eds. *Spiritual and Anabaptist Writers: Documents Illustrative of the Radical Reformation*. Library of Christian Classics 25. Philadelphia: Westminster, 1957.

Williams, Rowan. *Christ the Heart of Creation*. London: Bloomsbury Continuum, 2018.

———. *Why Study the Past: The Quest for the Historical Church*. Grand Rapids: Eerdmans, 2005.

Willimon, William H. "God Bless you, Mrs. Degrafinried." *Cheiarin Century* 1019 (14 March 1984) 269–70.

Wink, Walter. *Engaging the Powers: Discernment and Resistance in a World of Domination*. Powers 3. Minneapolis: Fortress, 1992.

——— *Jesus and Nonviolence: A Third Way*. Minneapolis: Fortress, 2003.

Wise, Tim. *Dear White America: Letter to a New Minority*. San Francisco: City Lights, 2012.

Wolkan, Rudolf. *Die Lieder der Wiedertäufer*. Berlin: Behr, 1903.

Yoder, John Howard. "Armaments and Eschatology." *Studies in Christian Ethics* 1 (1988) 43–61.

———, trans. and ed. *The Legacy of Michael Sattler*. Classics of the Radical Reformation 1. Scottdale, PA: Herald, 1973.

Subject Index

Abigail, 10, 71
abortion, 54, 99–100
Abraham (Patriarch), 4, 20, 70, 75–76, 96, 117
Ackerman, Peter, 128, 130
activism, nonviolent, 65, 69–70, 82, 106–7, 110–14, 126, 128n31, 129–30. See also witness, nonviolent
African American church, 63, 86–87, 88–93, 97. See also black church
a Lasco, John, 43, 48–49, 51
Alexander, Michelle, 90n6, 101n25
American exceptionalism, 64
Amish, Old Order, 17, 26, 104–5, 139
Anabaptism, ix, 2–3, 39
    and Apocrypha, 14, 148–50
    as believers church, 62–63, 86–88, 102
    biblical interpretation, 5, 14, 69–70, 73–74, 86, 122–27, 130–31, 133–34
    and black churches, 86–103
    Christology, 27, 30, 34, 42–57, 144–47
    contemporary, 39–40, 64–65, 61–62, 105–6, 118–19, 122–25, 130, 133
    defenseless, 12, 26, 104, 108–10, 133–34
    Dutch, 3, 18, 20–21, 42–59
    ecclesial/ecclesiology, 27, 70, 104
    ecumenical, 12, 67, 84–85
    historical stream, 39–41, 66–67, 117–19
    Hutterites, 107, 150
    hymnody, 1, 12, 17–26, 151
    lectionaries, 13, 139–43
    and nature, 4, 80
    Moravian, 25, 107, 149
    Münster, 25, 43, 108, 122
    nonviolence, 12, 22, 28–29, 104–10, 122–26
    as Orthodox, 27, 34, 38, 78
    Philipite, 25
    radical, 84–85
    sixteenth-Century, 3, 27, 66, 73, 131
    South German and Moravian, 18, 149
    specific to Jesus, 24, 27–28, 34, 38–39, 66–68, 75, 84
    Swiss, 18, 22, 149
    theology, 18, 27–37, 78, 147
    and Trinity, 14, 19, 27, 33–38, 40, 46, 77–78, 94, 97, 144–47
    and women, 17, 25, 107
Anna Jansz, 21, 150
Anna of Oldenburg, Countess, 48
Anthony, Susan B., 130
Anselm of Canterbury. See also, Atonement, satisfaction
Aquinas, Thomas, 46
Aristide, Jean Bertrand, 126
atonement, 25, 58, 94
atonement, nonviolent, 94–95
    as narrative Christus Victor, 94–95
atonement, penal/substitutionary, 56
atonement, satisfaction, 94
    accommodates slavery, 95
    accommodates violence, 94–95
    God agent of Jesus' death, 94

SUBJECT INDEX

atonement, satisfaction *(continued)*
    and black theology, 95–97
    passive Jesus, 94
    models surrogacy, 96
    and womanist theology, 96–97
Ausbund, 12, 17–26, 151

baptism, 19, 27, 31–32, 34–36, 38, 42, 44, 53–54, 61–63, 80, 86–87, 107, 109, 118
    Christ's 33
    infant, 29, 48, 61, 87
Barth, Karl, 4n16, 10, 24, 58
Bedford, Nancy, 101
Belgic Confession, 44–45
believers church(es), ix–x, 1n4, 62–63, 65, 70, 85–88, 92, 98, 100, 102
    Canada vs United States, 63, 70, 87
Bible
    interpretation, 1, 12, 24, 44, 64, 66, 69–70, 72, 74, 83, 102, 110, 112–13, 124, 133
    two voiced, 92–93
Bilach, Hans von, 21
black church, 65, 85–91, 97, 101–2. *See also* African American church
black theology, 65, 76, 85, 93, 95–96. *See also* Cone, James H.; Carter, J. Kameron
Bogomiles, 42
Bosch, Sigmund, von, 19–20
Boyarin, Daniel, 82n17, 97
Boyd, Greg, 11

Cafalan, Zaida, 130
Carter, J. Kameron, 13, 96. See also Cone, James Hl; black theology
Cathars, 42
Catholic/Catholicism, 3, 14, 24, 28, 32, 38, 48, 63, 85, 108
Chalcedon. *See* Christology, Chalcedon
chaos theory, 135
Charles V, 28, 32
Christian Nation, 64, 88
Christian Peacemaker Teams, 106, 126, 130

Christology,
    celestial flesh, 42–59
    Chalcedon, 49–51, 56, 77–78, 94–95
    Constantinople, 77
    Nicea/Nicene Creed, 77–78, 94–95
Church of God in Christ, 98
church and state, 98–100
Civil Rights movement, 69, 90, 114, 121–22, 128, 130
Civil War, 89
Clement Dirks, 3, 8
Cone, James H., 76, 90ng, 95–96. *See also* black theology; Carter, J. Kameron
Constantinople. *See* Christology, Constantinople.
continuum of violence/nonviolence, 119, 121–23
creation (biblical), 1, 5, 25, 47, 64, 71, 80, 82, 137, 150

David Joris, 48, 149
David (King), 10, 20, 71
defenseless Christians/church/Word, 12, 26, 108, 110, 133–34
Defenseless Christianity, ix, 61n1, 110n9
Denck, Hans, 4–5, 73, 107, 149
Dirk Philips, 43, 107–8, 148
disestablishment, 88n2
Dordrecht Confession of Faith, 104
DuVall, Jack, 128, 130

Enuma Elish, 71
Erasmus, 44, 61n2, 146
established church, 23–24, 27, 61–63, 87, 88n2, 104, 133, 135. *See also* mass church; state church
Eucharist. *See* Lord's Supper
evolution, 64

feminist theology, 85
flood, great, 71, 93
Finger, Tom, 27n1, 44
Force More Powerful, 128
forgiveness, 2, 10–11, 35, 76, 79, 81, 85, 112–14, 148
Fox, Tom, 130

SUBJECT INDEX

Franck, Sebastian, 23
Frankenthal disputation, 73
Froschauer Bible, 149
Friesen, Abraham, 44, 61n2
Funk, John, 44

Gandhi, Mahatma, 81, 128, 130
German Democratic Republic, 70
God,
    nonviolence of, 71–72, 74, 79, 92, 97, 117n15, 120
    violence of, 71–72
    See also Jesus, reveals God.
grain of the universe, 12–13, 64–65, 67, 78–83, 85–86, 91–92, 97, 103, 106–7, 110, 117–19, 123, 126–28, 131, 134, 136–37
    as wisdom, 82
Grebel, Conrad, 107, 149
Greene, Brian, 136
Grislis, Egil, 51, 56
Gulliver's Travels, 9

Hagar, 4, 76, 96
Haiti, 126–27
Hart, David Bentley, 82, 111
Hart, Drew, 90n7, 101
Hauerwas, Stanley, 12n28, 134
Het Offer Des Herren, 20
Hilary of Poitiers, 46, 146
Hoffman, Melchior, 43, 149
Holy Spirit, 30, 32–33, 35–38, 58, 137
Hubmaier, Balthasar, 149
Huldah, prophetess, 7
Hut, Hans, 4, 80

immigrants/immigration, 64, 118, 123
Into Account, 125
Irenaeus, 13

Jantzen, Grace, 13, 24, 137
Jennings, Willie James, 96
Jeroboam, kind of Judah, 9
Jesus,
    in Acts, 68, 70, 74, 76
    celestial flesh, 42–55

death, 10, 31, 38, 59, 64, 67–68, 71, 79, 82, 93–94, 96
    and ecumenical relations, 83–85
    and grain of the universe, 65, 78–83, 88
    as guide/norm, 14, 24, 27, 38–40, 61–62, 84, 88
    identified by narrative, 34, 38, 40, 66–68, 73–74, 76–79, 81, 94–95, 117
    healing withered hand, 112, 116
    liberator, 92–93
    mission of, 110
    and nonresistance, 104–6, 119, 122
    nonviolence of, 12, 29, 63, 69, 93–94, 104, 106
    and Old Testament, 70–78, 97
    reveals God, 1, 12, 18, 40–41, 92
    resurrection, 10, 31, 35, 37, 58–59, 64, 67–68, 72, 76, 79, 82, 92–95, 126–27
    and Samaritans, 78, 113–14, 116
    Sermon on the Mount, 78, 110–12, 140
    as source of theology, 76–78, 84, 93–97
    as spiritual seed, 18–20, 24
    submissive, 92–93, 95–96
    teaching, 115–16
    temple cleansing, 69, 78, 113–16, 121, 123, 135
    and women, 78–79, 116
    Word made flesh, 5, 6, 10
Joriaen Simons, 2–4, 7–8, 10
Joseph, 9–10
Josiah, king of Judah, 1, 7–9

Kaufman, Gordon, 5, 7
Keeney, William, 45–46, 52
Khan, Badshan, 81, 127–28, 130
Ku Klux Klan, 89
King, Martin Luther Jr., 69, 90, 114, 121–22, 128, 130

Latin Vulgate, 1
Levine, Amy-Jill, 97

SUBJECT INDEX

LGBTQ, 64, 85, 100, 102, 118, 124–25, 127
Loosveldt, Pierijntgen, 146
Lord's Supper, 24, 29, 32, 34–35, 52–53
Luther, Martin, 2–3, 7, 25–29, 38, 40, 43
lynching, 89

Mantz, Felix, 22, 107
Marpeck, Pilgram, 12, 17, 19, 27–41, 73, 107–8, 149–50
   The Admonition, 34–36
   Concerning the Lowliness of Christ, 30–35, 37, 40
   Expose of the Babylonian Wore, 28–30, 28–30, 34, 40
   and Trinity, 27–41
   Reply to False Accusations, 54
   Reply to Micron, 44, 49
Marcion, 42
Martin, Dennis, 58
martyrdom, 1, 20, 22, 43, 62, 89, 108–9, 150
Martyrs Mirror, 1–3, 8, 14, 62, 78, 89, 104, 108–10, 134, 144–47, 150
Mary Joris, 3
Mary of Nazareth, 4, 18, 20, 42, 44–47, 49–50, 54–55, 135, 145
mass church, 61–63, 70, 84, 87, 90. *See also* state church; established church
Menno Simons, 6, 12, 24–25, 42–55, 57, 107–8, 148
   Christian Baptism, 53
   Foundation of Christian Doctrine, 52
   Reply to Micron, 44
   Very Plain and Discreet Answer, 44
Mennonite,
   and conflict, 124–25
   contemporary, 105
   Dutch, 42–45
   nonresistance, 69, 105, 119, 122
   nonviolent, 130
   peace church, 95
   theology, 94, 105
Mennonite Disaster Service, 118
Mennonite Central Committee, 118, 130
Micron, Martin, 43–44, 48–50

moral influence atonement. *See* atonement, moral influence theory
Moses, 4, 70
Mott, Lucretia, 130
Müntzer Thomas, 149

naaktlopers. *See* naked runners
naked runners, 107–8
Nabal, 10
narrative Christus Victor. *See* atonement, narrative Christus Victor
New Jim Crow, The, 59n8
Nicea. *See* Christology, Nicea/Nicene
Nonviolence/nonviolent,
   activism, 65, 69–71, 81–82, 98, 104, 106, 111–14, 117, 119, 121–31
   church, 58, 93, 98, 123
   creation, 71
   defined, 107
   love, 134–35, 137
   theology, 94–95, 105
   Word, 12, 118, 22–23, 41, 51, 59, 66, 110, 137
   See also, God, nonviolence of.

Obbe Phillips, 107–8
Old Testament,
   beginning of Jesus' story, 70, 72, 74–75
   violent imagery, 71–73
   nonviolent imagery 71–73
Oosterban, J. A., 24–25, 58
Overdam, Hans van, 1, 20–21

Pappenheim, Walpurga von, 17
Passau prison, 25
Paul, Alice, 130
peace church, 27, 9395, 97, 101, 105, 124, 127
Plener, Philip, 25
Puritans, 88n2

Quantum theory, 135–36, 138

racism, 64, 86, 89–90, 95–98, 101–3, 106
reconstruction, 89

Reformation, 7–10
    Anabaptist, 2–3, 61–63, 66, 85, 87, 89, 104, 107, 134
    Protestant, 1–3, 4, 25, 61–64, 85, 87–89, 104, 133–34
    Radical, 1–3, 42, 84
Reformed Church, 43–44, 48–50, 52, 73, 139
Rempel, John, 27n1, 35n30, 36
restorative justice, 81, 118
Riedemann, Peter, 80, 150
Rivera, Mayra, 13
Rothmann, Bernard, 34–35
Rovelli, Carlo, 136

Samaritans See Jesus, and Samaritans
satisfaction atonement. *See* atonement, satisfaction theory
Sattler, Michael, 73n6, 107, 134, 149
Scandal of the Evangelical Conscience, 56
Scharnschlager, Leupold, 73
Schleitheim, 107
Schmalkaldic League, 28, 32
Schneider, Michael, 25–26, 151
Schwenckfeld, Caspar, 35–37, 42
Sharp, Gene, 128–30
Sider, Ron, 56
Simon the Shopkeeper, 109, 122
slave, slavery, enslavement,
    biblical, 1–2, 4, 6, 9, 76
    United States, 89–93, 95–96, 114
spiritualists, 17, 23, 35, 48
Sri Lanka, 128
Stassen, Glen H., 106
state church, 48, 63, 84, 87–88, 100
Strasbourg, 28–29, 108
Strings, Jelis, 145
substitutionary atonement. *See* atonement, substitutionary theory
sword, 11, 12n28, 22–23, 27–31, 34, 38, 40, 50, 55, 57, 62–63, 73, 75, 78–79, 84, 94–95, 101, 104–5, 108, 110, 120, 137
Synoptic Gospels, 5n19, 14, 115, 135

Syrophoenician woman, 125

theodicy, 91–92
Trinity. *See* Anabaptism, and Trinity
two-kingdom theology 56–57, 93, 105–6
Tyndale, William, 2

Valentinus, 42, 47
Vermeersch, Hans, 144
Verduin, Leonard, 44
Vietnam War, 129–30
violence,
    in abortion, 99
    in atonement, 94–95, 137
    in continua, 121–22
    is cyclical, 75, 80, 89, 128, 138
    defined, 106–7
    national, 6, 29, 32, 50, 57, 69, 93, 119
    Old Testament, 7, 9, 11, 70–72, 138
    racial, 89, 92, 94–97
    against women, 100, 123–25, 127
    structural/systemic, 12, 70
Vleckwijk, Heerman, 145–46
voluntary church, 63
Voolstra, Sjouke, 53, 55

Walpot, Peter, 80, 150
Westmoreland-White, Michael L., 106
white church, 65, 85–87, 92–93, 97–98, 100, 102–3
white privilege, 86n1, 87, 90, 100–101
white supremacy, 12–13, 96, 103
white theology, 95
Williams, Delores, 76, 96, 129n31. *See also* womanist theology
Williams, Rowan, 46, 67
Winona Lake, 105–6
witness, nonviolent, 12, 27–28, 63, 65, 107–9, 117–23. *See also* activism, nonviolent
Wenger, J. C., 44
womanist theology, 76, 82, 85, 87, 91–92, 96–97, 129n31

SUBJECT INDEX

women, 44, 46, 64, 90, 96, 100, 102, 124, 127 *See also* Anabaptism, and women; Jesus, and women.
Word of God
   In *Ausbund,* 17–26
   creative/creating, 5–6. 18, 45, 51–52, 133, 135
   dividing, 6–8, 135
   in Dutch Mennonite theology, 42–45
   enlightening, 18
   force in the world, 106, 133
   God's forgiveness, 2
   as Gospel, 68
   as Grain of the Universe, 12–14, 64, 66–67, 80, 83
   guide for life, 3, 53, 133
   Jesus as Word, 4, 19, 25, 41, 68, 75, 84–85
   living, 4
   in Menno Simons, 45–59, 108
   as nonviolent, 22–24, 41, 50–51, 57, 59, 72, 106, 133–35, 137
   reconciling, 8–11, 126, 135
   as reliable ground, 20–21, 25–26
   reveals Jesus' life and teaching, 1, 4, 24, 53, 66–68, 75, 78–79, 84, 126, 134–35
   ss Scripture/Bible, 1–3, 68, 147
   as spiritual seed, 18–20, 42, 46, 52
   undivided, 57
World War II, 99n22, 105

Yoder, John Howard, 12n28, 79, 117, 134

Zurich, 22, 107

Scripture Index

OLD TESTAMENT

Genesis

1	5, 82
1–2	71
1:26	149
4:19	9
5:11	149
15	4
16:10–12	4
	9

Exodus

1	71
3:10–12	4
10:1–17	4

Leviticus

17:18	115

Deuteronomy

6:5	115

Joshua

1–11	71

Judges

7	71

1 Samuel

23	10
25	71

2 Samuel

8	71

1 Kings

13:1–4	9
13:15	9
13:16–19	9
13:24	9
13:29–32	9

2 Kings

6	71
22:16–17	
22:19–20	7
22–23	1, 1n4
23:17–18	9

2 Chronicles

34–35	1n4

SCRIPTURE INDEX

Psalms

7	149
7:15–16	75
9:15–16	75
37:14	137
85:8–10	138
85–11	138
103:6, 17	138

Proverbs

8:1–16	82
8:22–23	82
8:24–31	82

Isaiah

61	110

Daniel 71

Jonah 71

APOCRYPHA

Tobit 148

Judith

10:1–5	149

Wisdom of Solomon 71

1:7	145
2:23	148
5:15–16	150
11	149
12	149
13:1–3	150
15:14–19	150

Sirach 148

13	150
15:14	149
17:3	148
27	149

1 Maccabees

1–6	150

2 Esdras 148, 149

5:1–7	148
7:6–9	150
16:70–75	150

NEW TESTAMENT

Matthew

2	140
3	140
4	140
5	140
5:38	110
5:39	69, 111
6	140
7	140
8	140
9	140
10	6
10:35–36	6
11	140
11:15	5n19
12	140
13	140
13:1–23	137
14	140
15	140
16	140
18	140
20	143
21:12–13	113
22:1–14	69
22:21	99

SCRIPTURE INDEX

22:36–38	115
23	116
24	143
25	143
25::31–46	118
26	140
26:47–56	4
26:52	11
27	140
28	140
28:19	36, 61, 107

Mark

4:9, 23	5n19
7:29:30	125
11:15–19	113

Luke

1	143
1:26–38	4
1:46–56	4
2	143
4:18	110, 114
6:6–11	112
6:27	81
10	141
10:27–28	113, 115
12–13	142
13:14	112
14	142
14:15–24	69
14:35	5n19
16	142
17	142
18	142
19	142
19:45–47	113
19:46	114
20	142
20:25	115
22	141
23:34	11
24:27	70

John

1	6
1:10	82
1:14	66
2:13–16	113
2:15–16	135
3	73, 140
4	141
4:1–39	123
5	142
5:19	35
8	141
9	142
10	142
13:1–18	141
14	141
15	140
15:26	144
16	142
17	141
17:8	144
18:36	79, 114

Acts

1–2	141
2:14–39	68
3–4	141
3:13–26	68
4:10–12	68
5–6	141
5:30–32	68
7–8	141
9–10	141
10:36–43	68
13:17–41	68

Romans

3:20	123
6	140
8	141
12	142
13	30, 93, 143

1 Corinthians

2:26–28	13
3:11	85
5	140
10–11	141
13	26, 141
15	73

2 Corinthians

3:1	37
5:17–19	13
6	143
6:17	6

Galatians

2	142
5	141

Ephesians

2:13–16	10
3	141
4	141
4:4–6	36
6:5	92

Philippians

2	142

Colossians

3	142

1 Thessalonians

5	142

Hebrews

4	6
4:12	5
4:13	7
11	142
12	142
13	142

James

2–3	143
3:19	149
4–5	143

1 Peter

2	143

1 John

3	141
5:7	33
5:7–8	37
6:8	33

Revelation

5:6–13	133
14	141
20:2	19

www.ingramcontent.com/pod-product-compliance
Lightning Source LLC
Chambersburg PA
CBHW071457150426
43191CB00008B/1378